Twayne's United States Authors Series

Sylvia E. Bowman, *Editor*

INDIANA UNIVERSITY

Hart Crane

HART CRANE

HART CRANE

by VINCENT QUINN

Brooklyn College

 35

Twayne Publishers, Inc. :: New York

For
Esther

HART CRANE

by

Vincent Quinn

The author of *The Bridge* stands in the front rank of American lyric poets of this century. Hart Crane's poems are distinguished by an eloquence that readers invariably find compelling. Yet he also arouses perplexity. His mosaics of metaphor fascinate the reader but may leave him doubtful of their meaning and success.

This study aims at clarifying Crane's achievement. His belief that poetry is the expression of gratuitous intuition is discussed. Seeing him in the tradition of visionary poets helps the reader to understand his method of composition. His central theme is recognized to be a desire for absolute beauty and love. His melancholy and hopeful attitudes toward the realization of this desire are presented, and individual poems best illustrating them are explicated—including several difficult ones, such as "Lachrymae Christi," "Possessions," and "Recitative."

Crane's major works—"For the Marriage of Faustus and Helen," *The Bridge*, and "Voyages"—are thoroughly analyzed in separate chapters. In "For the Marriage of Faustus and Helen," Crane felt he had celebrated an idealistic theme in modern poetic diction. *The Bridge* urges a single vision of America's past that anticipates a glorious spiritual destiny for the individual and the nation in the future. Yet several elements in *The Bridge* fail to sustain its positive theme. "Voyages," a sequence of six lyrics about love and the sea, is the richest in imagery and the most persuasive of all Crane's poems.

The misgivings about Crane's romanticism expressed by his most influential critics—Yvor Winters, Allen Tate and R. P. Blackmur—are discussed, and a summary evaluation of Crane's achievement is offered.

Preface

IN THE THIRTY YEARS since Hart Crane's death, the importance of his poetry has been established. It stands in the front rank of twentieth-century American lyric verse. He is represented in anthologies, discussed in literary histories, and assigned in college courses. In addition, new readers invariably find him powerful and compelling. Yet this recognition has not reduced the perplexity that his work has always aroused. Acknowledgments of its brilliance are matched by uneasiness over its obscurity and by uncertainty about its success.

Several critics—spurred perhaps by Crane's own motto from John Donne, "Make my dark poem light, and light"—have helped to overcome these difficulties. Philip Horton's *Hart Crane: The Life of an American Poet* and Brom Weber's *Hart Crane: A Biographical and Critical Study* offer moving accounts of the poet's life. Crane's poetic sensibility has been discussed most incisively by Allen Tate, Yvor Winters, and R. P. Blackmur. There are also excellent essays on individual poems, particularly *The Bridge*, although the number considered in this way falls far short of the total, and each poem is usually explicated in isolation from the others.

This study of Crane's poems surveys his principal themes, analyzes his major poems, defines his attitude toward poetry, and discusses the judgments of his most important critics. The keystone of this book is the recognition that Crane looked upon poetry as the expression of gratuitous intuition and that the central theme of his inspiration was the desire for absolute beauty and love.

Crane's belief in the objectivity of poetic intuition—and, consequently, his place in the tradition of visionary poets—is the subject of the first chapter. His outlook is also related to the controversy in the 1920's between the logical positivists' contention that science alone can make meaningful statements about reality and the humanists' insistence upon the autonomous and equally valid contribution of art. Crane's method of composition and his attitude toward logic and clarity are explained.

The second chapter enumerates the themes that spring from his desire for absolute beauty and love. These themes cluster about negative and positive poles. Negatively, they express Crane's dissatisfaction with the ordinary conditions of life. He laments that society, family, friends, and his own behavior have failed to satisfy his deepest spiritual needs. The majority of his poems are in this vein: lyrics of disappointment and misery, grieved outcries against the impurity and impermanence of his experience. They are complemented and given their fullest significance by his positive anticipations of fulfillment: visions of stainless love and beauty. Some poems are dominated either by melancholy or hopefulness; others present both impulses and gain great power from the tension generated between them. The most successful poems expressing these themes are closely analyzed—for example, "Legend," "Praise for an Urn," "Lachrymae Christi," "Possessions," and "The Wine Menagerie."

Crane's first major poem, "For the Marriage of Faustus and Helen," is discussed in the third chapter. Completed in 1923, it was a cardinal step in his development. He valued it as an important technical and thematic victory: the achievement of a modern poetic idiom in the service of an idealistic theme. It was also his first long poem, more than a hundred and thirty lines. He rejoiced in his accomplishment, hailing it as "only a beginning" in which he had "struck new *timbres* that suggest dozens more, all unique, yet poignant and expressive of our epoch." On its impetus he experienced his first vision of *The Bridge*.

The fourth chapter is devoted to *The Bridge*. Crane regarded this poem as the proof and pinnacle of his career, and in all respects it is a major literary achievement. It has magnitude of size and intention. It employs several episodes in American history as analogues persuasive to the growth of spiritual consciousness in the individual. It urges a single vision of America's past that anticipates its glorious spiritual destiny in the future. Each section of the poem is explicated, and particular attention is given to passages indicative of Crane's lapses of faith in his vision.

"Voyages"—Crane's sequence of six lyrics about love and the

sea—is the subject of the fifth chapter. Each poem is discussed in detail, including its relationship to the entire sequence. These poems are, in this study, considered Crane's finest. More intimately personal than "For the Marriage of Faustus and Helen" and *The Bridge*, they touch a richer vein of imagery and also carry a more persuasive charge than the more ambitious poems.

The sixth chapter takes up the views of Crane's most influential critics—Yvor Winters, Allen Tate, and R. P. Blackmur. They focus their attention upon his visionary poetic and transcendental theme, and relate these convictions to the impulse of romanticism. They conclude that Crane became ensnared in the chronic romantic errors of self-indulgence, self-conceit, and literary obscurantism. This negative attitude is examined and found inadequate. At issue is the non-rational mode in which creative intuition manifests itself in Crane's work. These critics are so aware of man's tendency toward self-deception that they suspect the worst whenever reason is not clearly served. They oppose Crane's poetic because they fear encouraging the wanton indulgence of irrationality. To offset this anxious view, the more hospitable position offered by Jacques Maritain in *Creative Intuition in Art and Poetry* is presented. Maritain respects the power of the creative experience to penetrate reality to a depth beyond, but not incompatible with, reason. This viewpoint offers a more serviceable approach to Crane's poetry than the one held by his American critics. Finally there is a brief evaluation of Crane's achievement. The chief merits and limitations of his poetry are suggested.

In this study the canon of Crane's poetry is taken to be *The Collected Poems of Hart Crane*, edited with an introduction by Waldo Frank (New York, 1933). The paperbound edition now also available—*The Complete Poems of Hart Crane*, edited with a foreword by Waldo Frank (Garden City, N.Y., 1958)—offers the same text.

VINCENT QUINN

Brooklyn College

Acknowledgments

To those who have fostered this study: Professors Quentin Anderson, the late Richard Chase, Lewis Leary, and Mark Van Doren of Columbia University; Professor Jacques Maritain of Princeton University; the poet Willard Maas, and Professor Seymour Reiter, my colleague at Brooklyn College.

All quotations from Crane's poems are from *The Collected Poems of Hart Crane*. By permission of Liveright, Publishers, N.Y. Copyright: © R-1961, by Liveright Publishing Corporation.

Quotations from *The Letters of Hart Crane: 1916-1932*, ed. Brom Weber, copyright 1952 by Brom Weber and reprinted with his permission.

Contents

Chronology

1899   July 21, Hart Crane born in Garrettsville, Ohio, the only child of Clarence and Grace Hart Crane. During the next four years, the family moved to Warren, Ohio, where his father established a successful maple-syrup plant.

1908   The family moved to Cleveland, Ohio, where his father organized the Crane Company, a chain of retail candy shops.

1916   First publication: the poem "C-33" in *Bruno's Weekly,* a small Greenwich Village magazine. Was encouraged to continue writing poetry by Mrs. William Vaughan Moody. His parents began divorce proceedings. He came to live in New York City.

1918   Became an associate editor of *The Pagan.* Returned to Cleveland and worked for a few months in defense plants.

1919   Again in New York City, working at odd jobs. In November, moved to Akron, Ohio, to work in one of his father's candy shops.

1920-   Lived in Cleveland, working for his father and in
1923   advertising.

1923   Publication of "For the Marriage of Faustus and Helen," his first major poem. Began writing *The Bridge.* Returned to New York City. From this time Crane made his permanent residence either in New York City or among a group of people in the arts at Patterson, New York. During the following years he had various jobs but was frequently unemployed.

1925   Received a grant of money from the financier Otto Kahn for leisure to work on *The Bridge.*

1926   Wrote most of *The Bridge* while living on his grandmother's plantation on the Isle of Pines, Cuba. *White*

Buildings published. Most of the poems in this volume had already appeared in magazines.

1927   Worked in California for a few months as a private secretary.

1928   Traveled in Europe for several months on an inheritance
1929   from his grandmother.

1930   *The Bridge* published.

1931   Lived for three months with his father in Chagrin Falls, Ohio. In March awarded a Guggenheim Fellowship for creative work in Mexico. He took up residence in Mexico City.

1932   April 27. Leaped to his death from an oceanliner traveling from Mexico to New York City.

1933   *The Collected Poems of Hart Crane* published.

Hart   Crane

My word I poured. But was it cognate, scored
Of that tribunal monarch of the air
Whose thigh embronzes earth, strikes crystal Word
In wounds pledged once to hope—cleft to despair?

—"The Broken Tower"

CHAPTER 1

Literary Outlook and Technique

HART CRANE'S POETRY is evidence of the miraculous power of art. Its expression of longing and grief saddens the reader; yet its artistry is awesome and arouses joy. His work is an outcry of unsatisfied yearning for absolute beauty and love that by its eloquence gives rise to hopefulness.

The source of Crane's grief is no mystery, for his personal life was a thirty-two years' ordeal. The only child of estranged parents, he became the foil for their mutual antagonism. He was always involved in their troubles but never confident of their love. When only eighteen years old, he wrote to his father: "Please, my dear father, do not make the present too hard—too painful for one whose fatal weakness is to love two unfortunate people, by writing barbed words. I don't know how long we three shall dwell in purgatory. We may rise above, or sink below, but either way it may be, the third shall and must follow the others, and I leave myself in your hands."[1]

Unable to trust his family, he relied upon friends. However, his need was too great and his anxiety too sharp for the easy terms of friendship. Slights, real and imagined, were suffered in agony and followed by outrageous displays of petulance. Before long in his letters, as his biographer Philip Horton has written, "the words 'betrayal' and 'humiliation' began to appear more and more frequently in the slowly increasing vocabulary of his suffering."[2]

At odds with others, Crane also felt at odds with society. In the midst of the prosperous 1920's he found himself without a high school diploma, unable to hold a job, and often forced to turn to his parents and friends for support. He pitied himself and lamented: "I am tied to the stake—a little more wastefully burnt every day of my life while all America is saying, 'every day I am growing better and better in every way.'"[3]

The combination of these circumstances and a passionate, violent temperament precipitated his addiction to homosexuality and alcohol. By the spring of 1932, while living in Mexico on a Guggenheim fellowship, he reached the climax of self-destructiveness. The novelist Katherine Anne Porter, who was living nearby, described an outburst of his despair: "He broke into the monotonous obsessed dull obscenity which was the only language he knew after reaching a certain point of drunkenness, but this time he cursed things and elements as well as human beings. His voice at these times was intolerable; a steady harsh inhuman bellow which stunned the ears and shocked the nerves and caused the heart to contract."[4] A few weeks later he leaped to his death from an oceanliner bound for New York.

I Dedication to Poetry

Hart Crane found life unbearable, but he was also a poet—and poetry is antithetical to destruction. A poet is constructive, a builder in words. He does not merely wish for beauty; he creates it. Writing poetry is an affirmation that precludes despair. The subject of the poem may be heartrending, the effort of composition may be an agony, but its deliverance is profoundly joyful to the poet.

Indeed, poetry was the single pure possession of Crane's life. He was humbly grateful for his talent, and by laboring to perfect it, realized his greatest dignity and satisfaction. He felt himself a member of a noble band whose calling demanded the utmost dedication and whose contribution to civilization was peerless. He once tried to explain to his father what it meant to be a poet:

I would like to just ask you to think some time,—try to imagine working for the pure love of simply making something beautiful, —something that maybe can't be sold or used to help sell anything else, but that is simply a communication between man and man, a bond of understanding and human enlightenment—which is what a real work of art *is*. If you do that, then maybe you will see why I am not so foolish after all to have followed what seems sometimes only a faint star. I only ask to leave behind me something that the future may find valuable, and it takes a bit of sacrifice sometimes in order to give the thing that you know is in yourself and worth giving. I shall make every sacrifice toward that end.[5]

He enjoyed practicing his craft and was proud of his accomplishments. "I am intensely,—grippingly interested in a new ballad I am writing," he wrote in the first of his published letters.[6] Several years later, following the favorable reception of his first major poem, "For the Marriage of Faustus and Helen," he rejoiced: "Allen Tate writes me the most glowing praises possible, calls me the greatest contemporary American poet, etc., etc., so I feel about ready to deliver myself of my memoirs and expire in roses."[7] While at work on *The Bridge,* he wrote to his friend Alfred Stieglitz: "[I was] simply carried . . . out of myself and all personal interests from the dot of five until two in the morning sometimes—for several days during which I was extremely happy."[8]

As long as he was doing a poet's work, he could maintain his self-respect. His dependence upon the dignity of the artist was made portentously clear in a letter written in 1924 to his mother: "The freedom of my imagination is the most precious thing that life holds for me,—and the only reason I can see for living."[9] Years later he faced the terrifying fear that drunkenness had robbed him of this freedom. His suicide was the seal of his despair that this "most precious thing" had been lost.

II *The Poet as Visionary*

Crane's joy at being a poet did not spring only from his satisfaction at practicing a constructive and honorable craft. It was drawn from a deeper source: his conviction that a poet is a seer, an inspired creature who is permitted a more profound glimpse into reality than men ordinarily experience. He associated himself with the long succession of visionary poets who have shared Plato's belief that

> all good poets, epic as well as lyric, compose their beautiful poems . . . because they are inspired and possessed. And as the Corybantian revellers when they dance are not in their right mind, so the lyric poets are not in their right mind when they are composing their beautiful strains: but when falling under the power of music and metre they are inspired and possessed. . . . For the poet is a light and winged and holy thing, and there is no invention in him until he has been inspired and is out of his senses, and the mind is no longer in him: when he has not attained to this state, he is powerless and is unable to utter his oracles. . . . not by art does the poet sing but by power divine.[10]

This conviction marks the tradition of Blake, Coleridge, Poe, Emerson, Baudelaire, Rimbaud—and Hart Crane. In this tradition the creative experience of the poet is regarded as a gratuitous visitation far beyond his conscious power and control. The poem resulting from this experience is a verbal report of an inspiration. This transformation of the poet from his ordinary self to the role of seer is what Rimbaud meant in writing *"Je est un autre"* in his first *lettre du voyant*.[11]

Crane believed that his poetic visions contained implicit knowledge about man and nature that could be obtained in no other way. He felt that these experiences offered an objective insight into reality. He shared the philosopher Jacques Maritain's view that the poet's intuition is "an obscure grasping of his own Self and of things"[12] and that "it is really and genuinely knowledge, though obscure and perhaps incapable of giving an account of itself."[13] From this point of view, the poet's vision is objectively valid, even though he experiences it through the channel of his subjectivity. Not only did Crane believe that poets are among the few human beings who realize their opportunity to make unique, interior discoveries about what exists, but he also valued poetry as virtually the expression of a mystical experience. He explained to his friend Gorham Munson:

> Poetry, in so far as the metaphysics of any absolute knowledge extends, is simply the concrete *evidence* of the *experience* of a

recognition (*knowledge* if you like). It can give you a *ratio* of fact and experience, and in this sense it is both perception and thing perceived, according as it approaches a significant articulation or not. This is its reality, its fact, *being*. . . . poetry, without attempting to logically enunciate such a problem or its solution, may well give you the real connective experience, the very "sign manifest" on which rests the assumption of a godhead.[14]

Crane considered himself the fortunate recipient of this aesthetic experience. It came unbidden, suffused him, and left him under the compulsion to articulate, however imperfectly, what he had experienced. It was a rich and powerful epiphany that he joyfully accepted but could not control. He saw himself as merely the channel or vehicle of an experience as real as breathing, but he could not "know" it until it had been defined in poetry. Once in a letter to Allen Tate, in which he had been outlining his differences with Eliot, Crane broke off to admit: "These theories and manoeuvres are interesting and consolatory,— but of course, when it comes right down to the act itself,—I have to depend on intuition, 'inspiration' or what you will to fill up the page."[15] Sometime later he wrote to Waldo Frank: "There is only one way of saying what comes to one in ecstasy. One works and works over it to finish and organize it perfectly—but fundamentally that doesn't affect one's *way* of saying it."[16]

Crane's goal was to make an equation between his creative intuition and the poem that sprang from it. He gauged his success by the adequacy of his words to what he already knew as experience. This relationship between the words he chose and prior non-verbal experiences explains the significance of an incident reported by Malcolm Cowley. Crane was leafing through a dictionary when he came upon the word "spindrift." He immediately recognized it as the right word for the last line of "Voyages II": "The seal's wide spindrift gaze toward paradise."[17] His choice of this word was not capricious; he had known that the line was wrong without it, even though he had not known the word he needed. Coming upon "spindrift," he simultaneously recognized its rightness and overcame the discomfort caused by his earlier unsuccessful efforts.

III *Artistic Principles*

The obligation to achieve a verbal equivalent for a unique experience demanded the utmost semantic freedom. The denotations of words had to be kept from overwhelming their far-ranging connotations. The restrictions of discursive logic had to be transgressed when they made experience less true to its actual complexity, even though more manageable. In an unpublished essay "General Aims and Theories,"[18] written in 1925, Crane stated that "the entire construction of the poem is raised on the organic principle of a 'logic of metaphor,' which antedates our so-called pure logic."[19] This principle allowed him to create a work adequate to the complexity of his intuitive experience. His poetry might violate ordinary logic and, to that extent, be nonrational, but it could not be antirational because it was governed by the same experience that reason handles with less completeness.

Crane recognized that practicing this principle made his poems frequently seem obscure and thereby limited his audience. His rejoinder was: "On the other hand I find [it] at times the only means possible for expressing certain concepts in any forceful or direct way whatever."[20] He wished to respect ordinary logic and syntax as long as he could also remain true to the experience that engendered the poem. He wrote to Allen Tate, "'Make my dark poem light, and light' . . . is the text I chose from Donne some time ago as my direction. I have always been working hard for a more perfect lucidity, and it never pleases me to be taken as wilfully obscure or esoteric."[21] Nevertheless, immediate clarity was not to be achieved by sacrificing the fidelity of the work to its intuition. When his intuition violated logic, Crane himself, along with his readers, had to be permissive and trust that its organic impact on the imagination would establish its coherence. He saw that this method might bemuse him into mistaking subjective confusion for objective illumination, but he accepted this possibility as an unavoidable risk.

These convictions placed Crane in opposition to the widespread belief in the twentieth century that poets are dreamers, wishful thinkers, and self-deceivers. According to this belief, poetry may support the psychological well-being of poets and their readers and may afford the pleasure of eloquence, but it cannot contribute to our knowledge of objective reality. This viewpoint was dramatically expressed in I. A. Richards' early book *Science and Poetry* (1926). He contended that, in so far as poetry adds anything new to our knowledge, it adds only the subjective experience of the poet. Science alone can make "true statements"; that is, statements with objective validity. Poetry is limited to the "pseudo-statement": "a form of words which is justified entirely by its effect in releasing or organizing our impulses and attitudes." Poetry is pleasing and service-able as long as it is regarded merely as the expression of subjective impulses and attitudes. If we think that it makes objectively valid statements, our use of it "has many analogies with drug-taking."[22]

IV *The Influence of Pound and Eliot*

In sustaining his faith in the autonomous value of poetry, Crane received tremendous encouragement from the critical writings of Ezra Pound. In what T. S. Eliot has called "the *least dispensable* body of critical writing in our time,"[23] Pound hectored poets, critics, teachers, and all other readers to take poetry seriously. Pound reminded them that "great literature is simply language charged with meaning to the utmost possible degree"[24] and that poetry is more significant than prose be-cause it carries a higher charge. Since human destiny is linked to the use of language, poets are the "antennae of the race."[25] They report the most essential news about the nature of man and reality. Upon the accuracy and depth of their statements depends the level of our self-awareness. In language deliberately chosen to play upon the modern reader's respect for scientific facts, Pound warned: "It is as important for the purpose of thought to keep language efficient as it is in surgery to keep tetanus bacilli out of one's bandages."[26]

He admonished poets themselves more sharply than readers. He saw the futility of badgering readers to look to poetry for precise reports on the human situation if poets were not able to give them. He protested to Harriet Monroe that "a man can get more for doing rotten writing than he can for doing rotten chemistry."[27] At times he despaired of teaching poets that theirs is an art that requires the work of a lifetime.

Pound also gave his testimony as a poet to the essentially gratuitous nature of poetic intuition: "The thing that matters in art is a sort of energy, something more or less like electricity or radioactivity, a force transfusing, welding, and unifying. A force rather like water when it spurts up through very bright sand and sets it in swift motion."[28] He added that "the poetic fact pre-exists."[29]

Perhaps of greater importance, Pound directed his readers to the modern French poets and critics who insisted upon the objectivity of poetic insight. In the work of Baudelaire, Rimbaud, Mallarmé, Verlaine, and Laforgue—poets introduced to Crane and many other American readers by Pound in *The Little Review* in 1918—this conviction was manifested with extraordinary intensity and sophistication. These poets reaffirmed the unique character of poetry's contribution to human understanding. They believed that poetic intuition consists of a fusion of the poet's individuality and the objective world and that the result—the poem—is as objectively true as the empirical observation of the scientist. This belief liberated them from the weight of scientific prejudice and heartened them to accept their subjection to the Muse with faith and pride. Their claiming a territory for poetry as independent as that of science has seemed to Jacques Maritain to have "a historical importance equal in the domain of art to that of the greatest epochs of revolution and renewal of physics and astronomy in the domain of science."[30]

Although Crane felt a debt of gratitude to Pound for reinforcing his intuitions about the nature of poetry, he was more deeply influenced by T. S. Eliot. Eliot's essays, the most forceful critical writing in English during the 1920's, encouraged Crane's respect for poetry in the same way as Pound and the French symbolist poets did. The famous analogy in Eliot's "Tradition and the Individual Talent" (1919) between the intuition of the poet and the action of the catalytic strip of platinum that changes the elements it is among and yet remains unchanged itself strengthened Crane's faith in the impersonality and objective validity of poetic inspiration. It is significant that in this comparison Eliot, like Pound and Maritain, refers explicitly to scientific material; he was pressing for the recognition of the distinct but equal claim of poetry and science to objectivity, and he felt confident enough to force the issue. His emphasis upon both the passivity of the poet during the experience of intuition and the independence of a work of art had the same intention.

In addition, Eliot focused attention upon earlier writers in English literature who provided a verbal intensity consonant with Crane's sensibility. In numerous letters Crane mentioned the writers he most admired—and always the reorientation of literary taste stimulated by Eliot is apparent. "More and more am I turning toward Pound and Eliot and the minor Elizabethans for values," he told Gorham Munson in 1919.[31] Two years later he explained the same predilection more fully:

> I've been having a wonderful time diving into Ben Jonson.
> . . . You have doubtless known my long-standing friendship with Donne, Webster, and Marlowe. Now I have another Mermaid "conjugal" to strengthen the tie. The fact is, I can find nothing in modern work to come up to the verbal richness, irony and emotion of these folks, and I would like to let them influence me as much as they can in the interpretation of modern moods. . . . I am not at all satisfied with anything I have thus far done, mere shadowings, and too slight to satisfy me. I have never, so far, been able to present a vital, living and tangible,—a positive emotion to my satisfaction. For as soon as I attempt such an act I either grow obvious or ordinary, and abandon the thing at the second line. Oh! it is hard! One must be drenched in words, literally soaked with them to have the right ones form themselves into the proper pattern at the right moment.[32]

Ultimately, the impact of Eliot's poetry upon Crane was so strong that it was troublesome. From his astute remark in 1920 that "Eliot's influence threatens to predominate the new English,"[33] all Crane's references to Eliot indicate the pivotal role the older poet played in his own development. In 1922, he wrote to his new correspondent Allen Tate about the problem of resisting being overwhelmed by Eliot's mastery:

I have been facing him for *four* years,—and while I haven't discovered a weak spot yet in his armour, I flatter myself a little lately that I have discovered a safe tangent to strike which, if I can possibly explain the position,—goes *through* him toward a *different goal.* You see it is such a fearful temptation to imitate him that at times I have been almost distracted. He is, you have now discovered, far more profound than Huxley (whom I like) or any others obviously under his influence. You will profit by reading him again and again. I must have read "Prufrock" twenty-five times and things like the "Preludes" more often. . . . In his own realm Eliot presents us with an absolute *impasse*, yet oddly enough, he can be utilized to lead us to, intelligently point to, other positions and "pastures new." Having absorbed him enough we can trust ourselves as never before, in the air or on the sea.[34]

V *Poetic Achievement*

The result of these efforts and attitudes is a body of work—*The Collected Poems of Hart Crane*—that stands in the vanguard of twentieth-century American verse beside the poems of Frost, Pound, Eliot, Williams, and Stevens. It is a small volume—fewer than a hundred poems, even if the sections of *The Bridge* are counted separately—but one marked by the eloquent rendering of a passionate, far-reaching imagination.

The earliest group of Crane's poems is *White Buildings*, a volume of twenty-eight lyrics published in 1926.[35] Containing poems written from 1917 to 1926, *White Buildings* offers a splendid sampling of Crane's lyricism. There are the best of his early work—poems like "Chaplinesque," "My Grandmother's Love Letters," and "Praise for an Urn"; his first major poem, "For the Marriage of Faustus and Helen" (1923); and the deeply moving, confessional lyrics of disappointment and hopefulness, like "Possessions," "Lachrymae Christi," "The Wine Menagerie," and "Voyages." The finest poems of this volume are explicated either in the next chapter, which discusses Crane's principal themes, or in the separate chapters on "For the Marriage of Faustus and Helen" and "Voyages."

Next is *The Bridge* (1930), his most widely known work and the one Crane regarded as the proof and pinnacle of his career. In all respects a capital literary achievement, it joins *The Waste*

Land, The Cantos, and *Paterson* as one of the most ambitious modern American poems. It has magnitude of size—fifteen sections extending over twelve hundred lines—and intention. As shall be seen in the analysis of *The Bridge* in Chapter IV, Crane ranges over the entire span of American history in urging a single vision of the past that anticipates the nation's glorious spiritual destiny in the future.

Finally there are the single lyrics written after the publication of *White Buildings.* They are in two groups: *Key West,* a volume of twenty-two poems that Crane had ready for publication at the time of his death; and twelve poems found among his worksheets after his death and included in a section called "Uncollected Poems." These two groups generally reveal the darkening and weakening of Crane's talent.

The poems of *Key West* were written from 1926, when Crane was getting *The Bridge* under construction, through the four years he spent completing it, to the end of his life two years later. "The Broken Tower"—the finest poem of the collection—was concluded just a few weeks before his death in April, 1932. They are mainly poems of fear, written either when *The Bridge* was temporarily abandoned and he feared he lacked the faith or the talent to finish it or, following its publication, when he feared that he had failed and could not bear the thought of the future. In addition to "The Broken Tower," the best of these poems are "Key West," "O Carib Isle!", "The Idiot," "Royal Palm," and "The Hurricane."

The atmosphere of *Key West* is violent and alien to man. Reality is felt under the pressure of heat, storms, waste, and death; there is a frightening mingling of fecundity and desolation. Although sensuality is offered a gross and pointless parody of itself, its presence is so intense that faith in anything superior to it is discouraged.

Crane conceived many of these poems under the influence of such a climate; they were occasioned by his experiences on the Isle of Pines (Cuba) and in Mexico. The others, written elsewhere, express what might be called a tropical state of mind. Crane was losing his battle to preserve an idealistic vision in the midst of a sensual jungle. His self-awareness remained clear and honest, but it doomed him to the consciousness of imminent defeat.

According to Waldo Frank, the twelve "Uncollected Poems" "were found in manuscript among the poet's papers, and were written for the most part in the last three or four years of his life. . . . Many of them, it is clear, are incomplete and were so considered by the poet."[36] They express the same temper as *Key West*: several were occasioned by Crane's experiences in Cuba and Mexico, and all reflect his isolation, defeat, and weariness. Only "The Visible the Untrue" seems on a level with Crane's representative work.

Altogether, Crane's poems present an unusually powerful lyric voice. Its identifying feature is his brilliant command of metaphor. His imagination fixed upon images of tremendous energy. It is remarkable how many of his readers remember some particular phrase with awe and pleasure. It may be the description of the sea gulls in "To Brooklyn Bridge"—"shedding white rings of tumult"—or the snake recalled in "Van Winkle"—"some sunning inch of unsuspecting fibre"—or the apostrophe to the Brooklyn Bridge in "Atlantis":

> O Thou steeled Cognizance whose leap commits
> The agile precincts of the lark's return

We may recall any of a multitude of images from "Voyages": the ocean as "this great wink of eternity," the mystery of "the seal's wide spindrift gaze toward paradise," or the tender mercies of the sea:

> where death, if shed,
> Presumes no carnage, but this single change,—
> Upon the steep floor flung from dawn to dawn
> The silken skilled transmemberment of song

These charged and rhythmical images constitute the magnificence of Crane's poems; their abundance often creates a bewilderment of plenty. A succession of compressed, richly connotative images accompanied by little or no discursive statement—as in "Lachrymae Christi"—dazzles the reader but may leave him uncertain in his response. He may feel that the poem possesses a unity that he has not been able to discover. The form of the poem is usually familiar—frequently blank verse arranged in quatrains—but the images may not seem to cohere.

This difficulty results from Crane's particular sensibility and his poetic theory. His imagination was vividly responsive to the associations of images: connotations that often lie below the threshold of consciousness. He thought and felt in images; his references to a logic of metaphor accurately describe his intellectual equipment. Moreover, he believed poetry to be the concrete evidence of an experience. The poet was not to tell about an experience but to convey it to the reader in the sensual terms in which he had received it.

The sure remedy for any perplexity caused by this poetic is rereading. The pleasure taken in one image may be employed as the motive for reading the entire poem again. On each reading, if the reader patiently suspends his desire for immediate clarity, further details assume significance and begin to illuminate others until the entire poem has been apprehended. In turn, the grasp of one poem enhances the reading of another until the entire collection is seen as a mosaic by a single artist.

CHAPTER 2

Major Themes

I *Anxiety and Grief*

AS ALREADY INDICATED, unhappiness is at the core of
Crane's themes. A vein of misery runs from his earliest
poems to his last. His disposition is fearful; his relationships with
family and friends, melancholy; his attitude toward society,
hostile.

Several poems suggest a generally troubled, anxious temperament. In an early one, "In Shadow," the lover is relieved by
the presence of his beloved because, in the growing dusk of
the garden, it is "too late / To risk alone the light's decline."
In "Repose of Rivers," the poet recalls from his youth "the pond
I entered once and quickly fled." "Paraphrase" is a morbid
fantasy of dying in one's sleep and being found "already /
Hollowed by air," "a white paraphrase" of oneself "among bruised
roses on the papered wall."

Anxiety is expressed more successfully in "Poster," written
in 1922 and later published as "Voyages I." The weakness of his
other poems on this theme is that they suggest merely a personal,
childish terror. In "Poster" a universal relevance is attained by
his use of the sea to symbolize the unavoidable painfulness of
life. The poem is also strengthened by his dramatic invention:
the poet, whose innocence has been lost, utters a warning to
"bright striped urchins," who, "gaily digging and scattering" sand
and shells at the shore, are unaware of any danger.

> O brilliant kids, frisk with your dog,
> Fondle your shells and sticks, bleached
> By time and the elements; but there is a line
> You must not cross nor ever trust beyond it
> Spry cordage of your bodies to caresses
> Too lichen-faithful from too wide a breast.
> The bottom of the sea is cruel.

At the same time he knows that such a warning is never heeded. As he wistfully regards their still unspoiled joy, he suffers the foreknowledge of their inevitable discovery of suffering.

In choosing the sea as a symbol of the apparent benevolence masking the terror of life, Crane was especially fortunate. He used it for the first time in this poem and responded to it richly. It provided him with a metaphor that could bear the heaviest pressure of his own experience without becoming sentimental or eccentric. Its universal significance was quickened by his personal response but not overcome by it. His further exploration of the resilience of this symbol led to the "Voyages" sequence and to some of the best sections of *The Bridge*. It also drew him close to the earlier American writers with whom he was most congenial —Melville and Whitman. He felt this kinship and drew strength from it. Indeed, "Poster" reminds the reader of Melville's repeated contrast in *Moby Dick* between the safe, gentle life of the land and the dangerous, terrifying life of the sea.

Crane's fear of nature is more grimly expressed in two later poems planned for *Key West*—"O Carib Isle!" and "Hurricane." Both poems bespeak his astonishment at the violence of the tropics. In "O Carib Isle!" he is frightened by the predominance of waste and death. "The tarantula rattling at the lily's foot / Across the feet of the dead" vividly suggests his terror. He also observes that, although death abounds, there is no mourning. Life seems to be reduced to a wanton mingling of fecundity and destruction.

He wonders about the metaphysical implications of this stark drama. "Where is the Captain of the doubloon isle?" he asks. He questions the nature and even the existence of its creator. Ironically he ponders the "Commissioner of the mildew" with his "Carib mathematics"—the "blue's comedian host," "Satan"— and inquires: "Who but catchword crabs / Patrols the dry groins of the underbrush?" He seeks self-definition in terms of this revelation of nature.

> Let not the pilgrim see himself again
> For slow evisceration bound like those huge terrapin
> Each daybreak on the wharf, their brine-caked eyes;
> —Spiked, overturned; such thunder in their strain!

Desperately he seeks grounds for rejecting this crippling identification but, as no alternative is discovered, he suffers a vision of his disintegration: "I . . . / Congeal by afternoons here, satin and vacant."

"The Hurricane" presents a different but no more comforting view of nature. The violence of a tropical hurricane is evoked in couplets that burst furiously. Although the storm is addressed as God and Lord, it has no personal consciousness. It is absolute, raw power, lacking all awareness and discrimination. Everything is ripped and swept before it: "Naught stayeth, naught now bideth / But's smithereened apart!" Crane's use of archaic forms to suggest biblical usage—"Lo," "Ay," "Thou," "e'en"— and his reference to "Scripture" are both appropriate and ironic. They suggest the harsh God of the Old Testament, or even the apotheosis of nature itself. It is as though the whirlwind of the Book of Job were not subject to God's control but asserted itself blindly. One might address it as a primitive deity:

> Thou ridest to the door, Lord!
> Thou bidest wall nor floor, Lord!

The storm is saluted as a personal God, but its action belies its consciousness.

Undoubtedly, Crane's anxious forebodings were conditioned by his unhappy family life. His letters document his difficulties; his poems attest to them in that every reference to a family relationship is sad. In the "Van Winkle" section of *The Bridge*, the poet thinks of his youth:

> So memory, that strikes a rhyme out of a box
> Or splits a random smell of flowers through glass—
> Is it the whip stripped from the lilac tree
> One day in spring my father took to me,
> Or is it the Sabbatical, unconscious smile
> My mother almost brought me once from church
> And once only, as I recall—?
>
> It flickered through the snow screen, blindly
> It forsook her at the doorway, it was gone
> Before I had left the window. It
> Did not return with the kiss in the hall.

He refers with greater bitterness in "Quaker Hill" to his plight as the child of divorced parents. He must "shoulder the curse of sundered parentage, / Wait for the postman driving from Birch Hill / With birthright by blackmail." An early poem, "My Grandmother's Love Letters," describes the poet's attempt to draw closer to his grandmother by sharing in her youthful experience of love. Alone on a rainy evening, he tries to discover his "mother's mother, Elizabeth," in letters that have grown brown and soft over the years. He knows that:

> Over the greatness of such space
> Steps must be gentle.
> It is all hung by an invisible white hair.
> It trembles as birch limbs webbing the air.

In becoming aware of how precarious his quest is, he loses confidence. Difficulties become apparent and paralyze his desire. The task of realizing the original force of old letters that were but the echoes of passion seems too large. He feels that he would inevitably impose himself upon his grandmother's experience and thereby distort it.

> And so I stumble. And the rain continues on the roof
> With such a sound of gently pitying laughter.

His ambition has been blocked; the desire for human sympathy seems unable to surmount the barrier of subjectivity. Only the consciousness of failure survives his impulse toward fellowship.

A similar conviction of the unbridgeable gulf in even the most intimate relationship is expressed in "Stark Major." A couple conceives a child in the ecstasy of love, but dawn brings "the lover's death." Not only must the lovers part, but the still unseen child will prevent their complete reunion. The father must

> Walk now, and note the lover's death.
> Henceforth her memory is more
> Than yours, in cries, in ecstasies
> You cannot ever reach to share.

Crane's poems about friendship are equally melancholy. In "Praise for an Urn," one of the most successful elegies in American poetry, he confronts the fact of death with his desire for a lasting relationship. Several impulses incline him to believe in the presence of his deceased friend. There is his affection, of course, but also his recollection of the large spirit of his friend, mingling "the everlasting eyes of Pierrot / And of Gargantua, the laughter." In addition, he recognizes that all his friend's ideas were "inheritances," gifts from other minds, "delicate riders of the storm." Just as men of the past lived on in the consciousness of his friend, so his friend may live on in him. Most of all, there are the experiences they shared.

> The slant moon on the slanting hill
> Once moved us toward presentiments
> Of what the dead keep, living still,

Tranquil, moon-charged evenings intimated the immortality of the soul to both of them and directed their conversation toward this possibility. Under the spell of nature's serenity and their spiritual intimacy, all reality seemed united and harmonious.

Now the confidence they felt together collapses as the lone survivor faces the fact of death. The funeral with its bold assertion of lifelessness and, even more, the cremation of his friend break the poet's faith. He realizes that even while he and his friend had been speaking of immortality and believing that nature sustained their faith, the clock "perched in the crematory lobby" had been ticking ironically toward that moment of dissolution. The poet's faith in personal immortality cracks under the mechanical flux of matter.

His resolution of this conflict is plaintively uncertain. The funeral and its aftermath of loneliness have dangerously weakened the poet's confidence in a deathless relationship but not destroyed it. Images of his friend return insistently and by their invincibility keep his hope alive.

> Still, having in mind gold hair,
> I cannot see that broken brow
> And miss the dry sound of bees
> Stretching across a lucid space.

This slim basis for hope holds the issue in tension, but it is in discouraging contrast to the trust he has felt while his friend was alive. He can only assert his desire; objective support is not available. So the poem ends meekly. "Well-meant idioms" are all that remain of their earlier "assessments of the soul."

> Scatter these well-meant idioms
> Into the smoky spring that fills
> The suburbs, where they will be lost.
> They are no trophies of the sun.

He fears that the same ashen fate that claimed his friend's body will be suffered—and perhaps deserves more to be suffered—by his poetic tribute to "what the dead keep, living still."

Crane's other poems about friendship speak of infidelity and alienation. The most poignant of these is "Voyages V." As we shall see later, the poet, having "dreamed / Nothing so flagless as this piracy," must endure being abandoned by his friend. This loss occasions his wistful yearning in "Voyages VI" for an "unbetrayable reply / Whose accent no farewell can know."

Crane's references to society reflect the same unhappy strain. Disappointed by family and friends, he is repelled by the harsh, materialistic ways of his era. In two sections of *The Bridge*—"The River" and "The Tunnel"—he expresses his revulsion. "The River" presents a kaleidoscopic nightmare of advertisements seen from a transcontinental railroad:

> SCIENCE—COMMERCE and the HOLYGHOST
> RADIO ROARS IN EVERY HOME WE HAVE THE
>   NORTHPOLE
> WALLSTREET AND VIRGINBIRTH WITHOUT
>   STONES OR
> WIRES OR EVEN RUNing brooks connecting ears
> and no more sermons windows flashing roar
> Breathtaking—as you like it . . . eh?
>   So the 20th Century—

In "The Tunnel" chaos is represented by a subway descending beneath the East River. Disconnected tags of vulgar conversation mingle with gongs, hissing doors, and cars screaming around curves. The poet feels "caught like pennies beneath soot and

steam," and he identifies his spiritual agony with the torment of
Edgar Allan Poe:

> And why do I often meet your visage here,
> Your eyes like agate lanterns—on and on
> Below the toothpaste and the dandruff ads?
> —And did their riding eyes right through your side,
> And did their eyes like unwashed platters ride?
> And Death, aloft—gigantically down
> Probing through you—toward me, O evermore!

Feeling alien to these conditions, the poet in "Chaplinesque"
identifies himself with the lonely, abused tramp of the movies
and uses him to symbolize the fate of human values in his time.
The familiar cop who always chases Charlie away from some
innocent enjoyment represents society. His prohibiting thumb
is "inevitable"; he sees life through a "dull squint" and opposes
all more liberal views.

II *Serenity through Suffering*

Upon this foundation of unhappiness, Crane strived for fulfillment and joy. In his personal life his hopefulness persisted almost
to the end—his resolution was "to keep saying 'YES' to everything
and never be beaten a moment, and I shall, of course, never be
really beaten."[1] Similarly, in his poems a dominant theme is his
faith in the possibility of happiness. "The poetry of negation is
beautiful," he wrote to Allen Tate early in his career, "alas, too
dangerously so for one of my mind. But I am trying to break
away from it. Perhaps this is useless, perhaps it is silly—but one
does have joys."[2] Sometime later he epitomized this guiding
impulse of his life and work: "I cry for a positive attitude!"[3]

His ability to aspire to happiness in the midst of misery
depended upon his trust that suffering may be the gateway to
peace. He believed that pain might be redemptive and enlighten-
ing, that "between black tusks the roses shine," as he wrote in
"The Wine Menagerie." Believing that the brave endurance of
suffering can instigate profoundly satisfying insights, he expressed
this faith in several poems about triumphant sufferers, most
notably about Jesus, in "Lachrymae Christi." Although this

poem has been considered "probably the most esoteric of all" by Philip Horton,[4] its theme becomes clear as soon as the reader recognizes that the sufferings of Christ, the birthpangs of spring, and the anguish of the poet are presented as analogous instances of torment. From this gathering of pain, a chorus of triumph emerges.[5]

A modern setting is established in "Lachrymae Christi" by describing the appearance of a factory in moonlight. The function of this image is to contrast the lifelessness of industry with the vitality of nature. "Benzine," a modern disinfectant and cleaning compound—the industrial equivalent of the tears of Christ—rinses the factory and "sluices . . . one unyielding smile" from its windows. The factory participates passively and fruitlessly in the redemptive passion of spring. At the same time, nature is undergoing the agony of regeneration. Rebirth necessitates pain and violence.

> Immaculate venom binds
> The fox's teeth, and swart
> Thorns freshen on the year's
> First blood.

However, suffering is only a minor counterpart to the positive value of spring. Though release from the coldness of winter is painful, the new season is joyful. Nature seems to be breaking into song, and men feel spiritually reborn. Nature's regeneration is man's sacrament of baptism; past failures are obliterated and purity is re-established. The nights "chant pyramids," symbols of spiritual ascent, and "anoint with innocence." The defeats of winter, the "perjuries" that had galvanized the eyes, are retrieved; and man's spirit is recalled to music. All creation—man and nature—joins in joyful harmony at rebirth. The theme is "not penitence / But song." At this point, Christ is invoked. The "distilling clemencies" of rebirth are identified with His redemptive tears: "these / Perpetual fountains, vines,— / Thy Nazarene and tinder eyes."

Crane then interrupts his celebration of rebirth to offer his personal testimony. He tells what a redemptive effect the tears of suffering have had upon himself: "Let sphinxes from the ripe /

Borage of death have cleared my tongue / Once and again." He
is released from the paralysis of his degradation as "some sentient
cloud / Of tears flocks through the tendoned loam." The self-
betrayed "stones" of his human soil may now "slowly speak."

This personal testimony is followed by a prayer to Christ, who
symbolizes the suffering by which the world is saved. He animates
nature whose throes in spring are epiphanies of His passion.

> Names peeling from Thine eyes
> And their undimming lattices of flame,
> Spell out in palm and pain
> Compulsion of the year, O Nazarene.

The concluding stanza is a supplication for the continuance
of Christ's redemptive act. He is beseeched to "lean long" from
the bleak beams of his cross and to "lift up in lilac-emerald
breath the grail / Of earth again." He is addressed as Dionysus,
the god whose self-sacrifice brought eternal life to his followers.
Homage is paid to His smile, world-redeeming, in contrast to
the "unyielding" smile of the modern god of industry.

> Lift up . . . . . .
>
> .   .   .   .
>
>   Thy face
> From charred and riven stakes, O
> Dionysus, Thy
> Unmangled target smile.

Less fervid but thematically similar to "Lachrymae Christi"
is "At Melville's Tomb."[6] Melville is praised for having borne
the torments of human experience with honesty and courage. He
did not coddle himself with illusions; he dared to face the terror
of life. He watched "the dice of drowned men's bones" sink
to obscurity on the shore, and he saw in the inhuman silence of
floating wrecks—

> The calyx of death's bounty giving back
> A scattered chapter, livid hieroglyph,
> The portent wound in corridors of shells.

Melville sought for the meaning of violence, and at last his perseverance was rewarded. The "lashings" of nature and his "malice" toward them were reconciled. His search became its own sanctification; in looking for meaning beyond the chaos of phenomena, he became aware of man's power to see beyond it. In struggling to understand violence, he took the essential step toward its transformation.

> Frosted eyes there were that lifted altars;
> And silent answers crept across the stars.

The nature of Melville's insight is not suggested, but confidence is expressed in his having achieved serenity. He became superior to the assaults of the elements. Now, in death, "this fabulous shadow only the sea keeps." His spirit dwells in the element through whose physical terrors he penetrated to peace.

III *The Creative Agony of the Artist*

Crane associated the achievement of serenity through suffering with the creative agony of the artist. He regarded his poetry as the justification for his life as well as the fulfillment of his literary talent. His sufferings were to lead to higher insights which would be fully realized only when expressed in poems. Crane attempted to illustrate this relationship between wisdom and art in all his poems, and he made it the subject of several. Among the best of these are two that appear in *White Buildings*: "Legend," and "Passage."

"Legend," appropriately the opening poem of *White Buildings*, announces the theme of the entire volume: artistic intuitions occasioned by suffering point the way to a higher positive view. The poem begins by presenting an image of the apparently inscrutable flux of experience. "As silent as a mirror is believed / Realities plunge in silence by." Like the spectacle of a waterfall to a deaf person, life passes without yielding its meaning. This incessant plunge of phenomena contains the "realities," but its inner significance is not easily understood.

The next stanza shifts to the poet's personal situation. He confesses that his experience with "reality" has been painful and intimately involved with his quest for love. Nonetheless, he remains steadfast in his struggle. In contrast to some of his contemporaries who have also found experience dissatisfying, he declares: "I am not ready for repentance; / Nor to match regrets." He has been hurt, but his injuries have sprung from his genuine response to the appeal of life. He has neither evaded nor forced experience. Moreover, he remains drawn to "the still / Imploring flame." Bravely he asserts that "kisses are,— / The only worth all granting."

His ambition is to fathom the experiences that thus far have hurt and baffled him. He accepts the self-surrender and suffering that the continuation of his search will entail.

> It is to be learned—
> This cleaving and this burning,
> But only by the one who
> Spends out himself again.

He anticipates the agony in terms of fire and blood, but he resolves to endure it "twice and twice / . . . and yet again"; for from its heart of pain a higher insight and reconciliation will come. He then enjoys a vision of his ultimate triumph. He will know "the bright logic" that surpasses ordinary, shadow-darkened conceptual understanding. It will break upon him with conviction and silence as the mystery of reality had previously—"unwhispering as a mirror / Is believed."

He foresees the relationship between his insight and his creative experience. The higher positive vision will be realized fully only when it is objectified in art. Realization and objectification will occur simultaneously. The pain, "drop by caustic drop," of deep seeking into reality shall wrench from him "a perfect cry" of "constant harmony." The moment of his outcry at the torment of his quest will be the moment of its fulfillment, for pain, vision, and artistic expression are inseparable. This expression of illumination will not only complete the poet's quest but will exercise an irresistible influence upon sympathetic readers. It will provide a "relentless caper for all those who step / The legend of their youth into the noon." The timid may find it bewildering and unattractive, but braver ones will respond gratefully to its harmony.

The temptation to escape from the painfulness of creativity is the subject of "Passage." The creative life seems monstrous at times, an imprudent exposure to terror. Compared to this danger-ous invasion of reality, the passive acceptance of life appears attractive. In "Passage" this easier way is suggested by the recol-lection of a visit to the country. The poet felt reprieved from the agony of city life which he associates with unhappy experiences and with the struggle to fulfill them in art.

> Where the cedar leaf divides the sky
> I heard the sea.
> In sapphire arenas of the hills
> I was promised an improved infancy.

Rejuvenation had a high price, however. Memory, the guardian of his previous experience with reality, had to be "left in a ravine." Abandoning it seemed largely a relief; it had been a "casual louse that tissues the buckwheat" and that "wakens alleys with a hidden cough," but a sacrifice was entailed also. Memory prolongs pain, but it also preserves joy and beauty; it "aprons rocks, congregates pears / In moonlit bushels." Yet, for a season the poet "joined the entrainments of the wind." He gave himself to the influence of the sun and rain.

Soon nature lost its appeal. The poet saw that it cannot satisfy man's needs. The struggle for human fulfillment may involve shame and suffering, but it is better than vegetation. The poet reluctantly resumed the burden of his humanity.

> . . . the wind
> Died speaking through the ages that you know
> And hug, chimney-sooted heart of man!
> So was I turned about and back, much as your smoke
> Compiles a too well-known biography.

He returned to the dark passions of man. He went to retrieve his discarded book of memory and found it, significantly, beneath a laurel tree in the grasp of a thief, Time. Understanding the grief that a decision to accept the human condition involves, Time asked, "Why are you back here—smiling an iron coffin?" The poet replied that he had come "to argue with the laurel," to attempt once more the transformation of human experience in art.

His resolution was immediately rewarded by a vision. As though to confirm him in his decision and to encourage him to greater effort, his resumption of the struggle with time and human nature was accompanied by a glimpse of a timeless realm.

> . . . from the Ptolemies
> Sand troughed us in a glittering abyss.
> A serpent swam a vertex to the sun
> —On unpaced beaches leaned its tongue and drummed.

He strained to catch the message. "What fountains did I hear? what icy speeches?" He failed; his memory was too earthbound, too "committed to the page." His new task would be to recapture this vision and to be adequate to its intensity.

IV *Grounds for Hopefulness*

Related to these themes is Crane's persistent faith in the joyfulness of love. He knew that love means suffering through self-surrender and that it involves the risk of betrayal, but he also believed its requital to be the supreme fulfillment of body and spirit. His noblest aspirations and his strongest creative intuitions centered upon the articulation of this conviction. In the "Atlantis" section of *The Bridge*, the sublime role of "the bridge" is to persuade men to accept the guidance of love in diverting their energies from mundane to spiritual satisfactions.

> O Thou steeled Cognizance whose leap commits
> The agile precincts of the lark's return;
> Within whose lariat sweep encinctured sing
> In single chrysalis the many twain,—
> Of stars Thou art the stitch and stallion glow
> And like an organ, Thou, with sound of doom—
> Sight, sound and flesh Thou leadest from time's realm
> As love strikes clear direction for the helm.

Similarly, as we shall see in detail later, the "Voyages" sequence is a celebration of the transforming power of love. "Permit me voyage, love, into your hands" is the theme of the entire poem. Its metaphor is the sea, and its movement is from the lover's dedication to a human and therefore changeable lover to a beloved beyond time and change.

Crane was even optimistic enough at times to see traces of nobility in contemporary society. He believed that America had become a slave to materialism, but he contended that this condition was not in keeping with either its finest tradition or the needs of human nature. He felt that his need as a person and his opportunity as a poet were to demonstrate a vision of life more worthy of the human spirit. Both "For the Marriage of Faustus and Helen" and *The Bridge* were intended to realize such a goal. "Faustus and Helen" asserts that even in the midst of urban chaos and the destructiveness of war a sensitive person may discover grounds for dedicating himself to love and beauty. Crane's purpose was to repudiate the nay-saying disparagers of his time and to offer instead encouragement to

> Distinctly praise the years, whose volatile
> Blamed bleeding hands extend and thresh the height
> The imagination spans beyond despair,
> Outpacing bargain, vocable and prayer.

The Bridge offers the same encouragement. The Brooklyn Bridge seemed to Crane the finest product of modern times. It not only represents the most advanced stage of technology and serves the most practical purpose but also satisfies the beholder's aesthetic and spiritual hunger. Crane saw it as an incarnation of beauty and a pledge of man's aspiration for the sublime. No man could see this bridge, he felt, and dismiss the age as vulgar.

On the impetus of this insight, Crane devoted the remainder of *The Bridge* to demonstrating the presence of similar evidences of idealism throughout American history. In each age he recognized signs sufficient to sustain faith in noble ideals. He hoped that the presentation of these signs would quicken his readers' faith in the fundamental spirituality of society.

V *Ideals and Experience*

As we might expect, Crane's combination of unhappiness and hopefulness creates considerable tension in his work. In the following chapters on "For the Marriage of Faustus and Helen" and

The Bridge this conflict will be discussed in terms of his attitude toward society. In these poems his wish for an affirmative view and his candor in presenting his melancholy impressions cause some disharmony between the theme and the tenor of certain passages.

This conflict is intense also in several of the shorter lyrics. In them he made clear that, although his strongest desire was to enjoy the happiness of love and creativity, he feared that he had failed to do either. He felt that he had sacrificed love to lust and that his creative skill had not grown properly. Yet, even in his most melancholy utterances, hope persists.

Although his involvement in the ordeal of love is most brilliantly expressed in "Voyages," it is also the subject of three other lyrics containing extremely concentrated images. They are "Possessions" and "Recitative," included in *White Buildings,* and "The Visible the Untrue," one of the poems found in manuscript after his death and included by Waldo Frank among the "Uncollected poems." All deal with the conflict of love and lust. "Possessions" is about a tryst that the poet foresees will end in the isolation of lust. Yet, even while anticipating failure, he pledges his continuing faith in "the pure possession" that someday will requite his desire for love.

"Possessions" begins—"Witness now this trust"—as the poet taunts himself for entering upon an affair that will almost certainly end in debauchery. Still, his hope persists that each new relationship will transcend fleshliness. He stands at the threshold with "the key, ready to hand—sifting / One moment in sacrifice (the direst)." He is prepared for the self-surrender required by love. Wistfully he contrasts the ease with which the doorkey finds its bolt with the uncertainty with which "through a thousand nights the flesh / Assaults outright for bolts that linger / Hidden." His spiritual quest must fumble in the darkness of sensuality as though heaven had "no eyes / For this fixed stone of lust."

Anticipating sexual intimacy, he enters to take up the stone of lust submissively but not blindly. He knows the difference between it and the ideal union he is seeking. Deliberately he sharpens this awareness by holding his lust up "against a disk of light." This action occasions a vision of his enslavement to passion and of his fellowship with all those whose ideals go unfulfilled. He expresses his torment in the imagery of a modern inferno:

> I, turning, turning on smoked forking spires,
> The city's stubborn lives, desires.

The "smoked forking spires" evoke another image of a victim of carnality. He sees himself as a stricken matador "tossed on these horns." The city image—"forking spires"—the perversion of the heaven-seeking church tower, and the nature image of the horns of a bull gather their implications of debauchery and bestiality into an outcry of tortured eroticism. The impaled victim "bleeding dies" and then suffers the worst anguish: he recognizes that, except for "piteous admissions," he has achieved nothing. The record of his quest amounts only to a "blind sum" and then breaks into self-consuming flame. It has consisted of "rage and partial appetites" but of nothing that will endure. Still, the poet's confession of failure does not destroy his faith in his ultimate success. He has yielded to impure possessions; "the pure possession, the inclusive cloud / Whose heart is fire shall come." This pure possession will purge away the stain of impure ventures; then will "the white wind raze / All but bright stones wherein our smiling plays."

In "Recitative" Crane universalizes his intimate personal conflicts and relates them to contemporary society. He recognizes aspirations and defections, communion and isolation, and elevated human consciousness and bestiality as the poles between which the human struggle rages. The resolution is a firm though humble affirmation of the possibility of wholeness and harmony.

Crane's handling of this theme in "Recitative" has generally been considered impenetrable. When his friends complained of its obscurity, Crane granted the complaint and tried as usual to help them overcome it. He pointed out that the only special difficulty in the poem is in locating the point of view, the dramatic context within which it is spoken. He had been compelled to keep this feature indeterminate because he wished to express several relationships simultaneously. His aim had been to extend the scope of the poem without jeopardizing its unity and force. He readily explained the several dimensions he had hoped to establish:

> Imagine the poet, say, on a platform speaking it. The audience
> is one half of Humanity, Man (in the sense of Blake) and the
> poet the other. ALSO, the poet sees himself in the audience as
> in a mirror. ALSO, the audience sees itself, in part, in the poet.
> Against this paradoxical DUALITY is posed the UNITY, or the
> conception of it (as you got it) in the last verse. In another sense,
> the poet it *talking to himself* all the way through the poem.[7]

This involved explanation probably made the poem seem even
more impenetrable because all these relationships could not be
located explicitly in the poem. What does come through—and it
is the point of Crane's commentary—is that the poem is not
merely personal. He intended to establish the universal significance of his self-knowledge.

His intention of probing beneath the surface of human behavior
is announced at the outset:

> Regard the capture here, O Janus-faced,
> As double as the hands that twist this glass.

He calls himself (and Everyman) "Janus-faced"—the god with
two faces—and he invites the reader to inspect him. This
ambiguity and its universality are stressed in the second line.
Pairs assert themselves: Janus, "double," "hands," and the mirror.
Everyone's inner and outer, darker and lighter aspects are seen
in the twisting mirror. The poet sees himself and shows his
image to all; he sees other men and shows them their own
reflection. Everyone sees more than his complacency usually
permits; the "speech" of these eyes is more than can be endured.

The core of the poet's revelation is separation, division.
Although men strive to preserve the illusion of harmony and
unity within and among themselves, the poet sees "twin shadowed
halves." Only their physical organism is of a piece; the psychological and spiritual life of every man is split by conflict:

> . . . and so it is
> I crust a plate of vibrant mercury
> Borne cleft to you, and brother in the half.

A broken mirror is an apt symbol of man. It reflects the
cleavages and incongruities so common that they even constitute

a bond of fellowship. In his divisions each man is his brother's twin.

A closer inspection of the image in the mirror is invited. Deceit is discovered in "this much-exacting fragment smile." Even if the "drums and darkest blowing leaves" of man's passion are ignored, his inevitable duplicity is seen. His smile is "much-exacting" of others; his apparent candor demands the same in return. Yet he reveals only a fragment of his nature and conceals the rest.

At this point, Crane anticipates the dispiriting effect his revelation may have upon the reader and tries to forestall it. He interrupts his analysis to urge his listeners to "defer though, revocation of the tears / That yield attendance to one crucial sign." Tears—symbols of compassion—must not be denied because of man's disharmony. They are to be shed in sympathy for all men's imperfect nature. Crane's desire is to quicken this sympathy, not to blight it.

He then proceeds to the conflict between human ideals and lust. The rational faculty tries to control physical passion but fails: "the wind feasts and spins / The brain's disk shivered against lust." Man suffers a division between love and lust as sharp as that between day and night. In the darkness he has "an ape's face" but it is masked as "white buildings answer day."

The reference to the "white buildings" of dawn occasions a transition from personal to social conflicts, for the cleavage within man's psychic life corresponds to the separation between people. Urban life aggravates this condition and provides an appropriate image for its representation:

> Let the same nameless gulf beleaguer us—
> Alike suspend us from atrocious sums
> Built floor by floor on shafts of steel that grant
> The plummet heart, like Absalom, no stream.

Each person is pent in a tower that, despite its luxury, resembles a jail.

Just as earlier in the poem Crane interrupts his recitation of the weakness of the human condition so that he may encourage his listeners to compassion, he now shifts to an even more positive assertion. He claims that, despite all symptoms of personal and social schizophrenia, harmony is possible if the will for it is strong. This challenge is introduced by his defiant use of the verb "let" in two places: "let the same nameless gulf beleaguer us" and "let her ribs palisade." It is specified by his exhortation to freedom: "yet leave the tower." The images of self-confinement and of the confinement of urban life are overcome by two images central to Crane's affirmative belief: the bridge and the sea. "The bridge swings over salvage, beyond the wharves; / A wind abides the ensign of your will." The second line here directly contradicts the pessimistic recognition made earlier in the poem that "the wind feasts and spins / The brain's disk shivered against lust." Crane then offers an example of the reconciliation of disparate or isolated elements as a spur to the acceptance of his challenge: "In alternating bells have you not heard / All hours clapped dense into a single stride?" This vision of harmony is the height of his affirmation. From it, because of the recollection of the predominantly negative tone of most of the poem, he modestly descends as the poem closes: "Forgive me for an echo of these things," but he also repeats his encouragement to "walk through time with equal pride."

"The Visible the Untrue," although unpublished during Crane's lifetime, was written about the same time as "Possessions" and was dedicated to the friend who inspired "Voyages." Indeed, since it is a lament for the end of a relationship that had seemed inviolable, it was probably occasioned by the same circumstances alluded to in "Voyages V" and it may be read as a companion piece.

The poet says that he has been victimized because of his desire for a perfect love relationship:

> Yes, I being
> the terrible puppet of my dreams

Although he knows that human nature probably cannot achieve the relationship he seeks, he willingly runs every risk in its pursuit. Regardless of the "neighbor tabulations / with all their zest for doom," he is ready to offer himself—though "split in two"—to his beloved.

He realizes the agony to which he exposes himself; he wears "badges / that cancel all your kindness." As he stands at a window at dawn, he sees a "silver Zeppelin / destroy the sky"—an image which conveys the ambiguity of his predicament. It evokes an awareness of his suffering, but it also suggests love's pure realization. He is reminded of

> The silver strophe . . . the canto
> bright with myth . . . Such
> distances leap landward without
> evil smile. . . .

This luminous vision contrasts pathetically with the failure of his actual love affair. In his dejection he likens himself to the window weight hanging beside him "in its blind /partition." Similarly, the dawn that promises "always, always the eternal rainbow" serves now "to extinguish what I have of faith." It brings the poet only "the day, the day of unkind farewell."

VI *Alcohol and Poetry*

Crane feared also that as a poet he had been untrue to his vocation, especially because of his addiction to alcohol. At the start of his career, having discovered that drinking stimulated his aesthetic sensibility, he hoped to employ alcohol as an aid to creativity. Thus in his early poem "The Wine Menagerie" he dedicates himself to the experience and the expression of poetic ecstasy, and he pays tribute to the power of alcohol to assist him.[8]

He first describes the transformation of vision induced by wine. It "redeems the sight" and allows "a leopard ranging always in the brow" to assert "a vision in the slumbering gaze." He is then able to enjoy a special insight into experience. He demonstrates this capacity by employing it upon the barroom scene taking place before him. He watches a man and woman and recognizes that their relationship is more violent than they would admit. The man's smile is a forceps, and the movements of her eyes are mallets. While their struggle goes on, a boy comes in from the snow to order a can of beer. As the boy buys

drink for adults in the wintry city, the poet notices that "August
meadows somewhere clasp his brow."

These intuitions cause the poet to speculate about human
experience. He wonders, "What is it in this heap the serpent
pries" and "From whom some whispered carillon assures /
Speed to the arrow into feathered skies?" He tries to reconcile
so much earthliness, "this heap," with the undeniable intimation—
"whispered" though it be—that spiritual arrows may be launched
into "feathered skies." He perceives that the desire for spiritual
ascent and harmony is fundamental to human nature. Whatever the cost, men naturally seek to overcome human limitations.
"Each chamber, transept, coins some squint, / Remorseless line,
minting their separate wills—." He is awestruck at the ability
of this desire to persist despite torment and frustration. He
watches "poor streaked bodies wreathing up and out, /
Unwitting the stigma that each turn repeals." Then he receives an intuition that expresses both the terror of this quest and the reward
for its completion: "Between black tusks the roses shine!"

His discovery of man's invincible wish for fulfillment turns
him back upon his own situation. He feels encouraged to plumb
his experience and to give formal expression to whatever he
finds. He celebrates the talent for intuitive understanding that
he feels growing within himself:

> New thresholds, new anatomies! Wine talons
> Build freedom up about me and distill
> This competence—to travel in a tear
> Sparkling alone, within another's will.

He foresees also the frustration he will endure until he has
fulfilled this talent. His task is to transform his whole nature
into a state of receptivity "wherein new purities are snared."
These purities are the idealistic tendencies that animate, however covertly, the behavior of all men. Even the tongues of
the damned have, he feels, at some time struck a higher note
of aspiration. Until he realizes this insight, any other success
will be paltry. Poems that fall short of this depth are only the
"frozen billows of your skill," he imagines his wit to protest.
He feels urged to free himself of ordinary preoccupations:
"Rise from the dates and crumbs." He must overcome the fear

of dissolution, the inevitable collapse of matter, and enter the undying realm of the spirit.

Later, as time brought him little recognition, Crane began to lose confidence in his talent. He drank more and more to relieve his depression and to invigorate his waning creativity. Gradually, alcohol became a tyrant, not a creative instrument. Aware of this calamity, he grew more melancholy and a more confirmed drunkard.

VII *Fidelity to the Muse*

The shame Crane felt at the collapse of his creativity is the underlying element in "The Idiot," which is included in *Key West*. He reproaches himself for failing to develop his poetic gift. The occasion is his watching a demented child whose absurd, unconscious behavior parodies his own. His description of the child is an ironic self-portrait that combines pity and remorse. He recognizes that he is more pathetic than the idiot, that at times the idiot sings more serenely than he has ever done.

The identification of the poet and the idiot is not explicit; it may even have been an unconscious self-projection. It centers at first upon the concept of the poet as a visionary. The boy is described as "daft / With squint lanterns in his head"; he holds a tin can "peeled and clapped to eye."

> That kite aloft—you should have watched him scan
> Its course, though he'd clamped midnight to noon sky!

They are both of ambiguous sexuality also—the boy is "likely / Fumbling his sex"—and both are rejected by society—"those children laughed / In such infernal circles round his door." They are linked, too, by the concept of the poet as a singer. Ironically, the idiot has achieved success, whereas the poet has failed. In the face of this turnabout, the poet feels ashamed:

> And since, through these hot barricades of green,
> A *Dios gracias, grac*—I've heard his song
> Above all reason lifting, halt serene—
> My trespass vision shrinks to face his wrong.

A more explicit presentation of this theme is achieved in "The Broken Tower." This powerful lyric conveys Crane's self-reproach for failing as an artist, but it also expresses his abiding faith in the sublime source of poetic intuition and in its involvement with love. "The Broken Tower" unites therefore the convictions, fears, and hopes of his entire career. It is an epitome of his outlook and eloquence.

The central image of the poem is the bell tower of a church, probably one Crane saw in Mexico City. The bell rope "gathers God at dawn" by calling worshippers to take part in the divine service. Unhappily, the poet feels unworthy of participating. Rather, as he returns from a night of sensuality—"feet chill on steps from hell"—the bell rope "dispatches" him as though he "dropped down the knell / Of a spent day." Despite his degradation, he still recognizes that the bells peal an exalted message. Their "shoulders sway / Antiphonal carillons launched before / The stars are caught and hived in the sun's ray."

The bell tower is broken, and it seems to the poet to be an image of himself. He has tried to be responsive to creative intuitions, but

> The bells, I say, the bells break down their tower;
> And swing I know not where.

As "their sexton slave," he has known their distressing and imperious power. Those who hear their "oval encyclicals" are spoiled for ordinary life by an irresistible and elusive calling. Serving them means a "long-scattered score of broken intervals." It consists of rare epiphanies of "pagodas, campaniles with reveilles outleaping" and desperate, inadequate efforts to echo their harmony.

He has dedicated himself to this ennobling slavery. He accepts his servitude, for it is fealty to a most dignified opportunity: the chance to be a poet. He is a vassal to creative ecstasy, "its voice / An instant in the wind (I know not whither hurled)" but bespeaking always "the visionary company of love." In his poems he has struggled to be loyal to this service, but he doubts that his words have been "cognate, scored / Of that tribunal monarch of the air." His wounds suffered in submitting to the "crystal Word" of intuition that "pledged once to hope" now seem "cleft to despair." He has received no confirmation of his intuitions beyond "the steep encroachments" of his nature that have betrayed him too often to be trusted.

From the impasse of an isolated sensibility turning suspiciously upon itself, the poet is rescued by love. Encouragement is offered by someone "whose sweet mortality stirs latent power." The poem is transformed from a dirge over his ruined career to a celebration of hopefulness. He feels "revived and sure," "healed, original now, and pure." He looks forward once more to becoming a channel of creativity. He is a new tower, more durable than the old—"Not stone can jacket heaven"—but composed of "visible wings of silence" that plumb "the matrix of the heart." He believes that love will conduct him to the spiritual realm that he has always sought but that he feared he had lost forever.[9]

An irony in keeping with the pathos of Crane's life is that this splendid and upward-looking poem was his last. He hoped it would be a turning point from the mediocre work he had done since *The Bridge*. In February, 1932, he wrote to a friend, "I've got to work on the first impressive poem I've started on in the last two years."[10] During the next few weeks he struggled to complete it. Its complexity of imagery and theme tested his skill rigorously, and he dreaded failure. He finished it and sent a copy to Malcolm Cowley. Unfortunately, an answer was slow in coming, and Crane interpreted silence as disapproval.[11] On April 27, 1932, he committed suicide, unaware of the high praise this poem would later receive.

CHAPTER 3

"For the Marriage of Faustus and Helen"

I *"New Timbres"*

THE COMPLETION OF "For the Marriage of Faustus and Helen" in 1923 was an important step in Crane's development. He spoke joyfully of it as "only a beginning" but one in which he had "struck new *timbres* that suggest dozens more, all unique, yet poignant and expressive of our epoch."[1] The critics whose opinion meant most to Crane—Allen Tate, Gorham Munson, and Waldo Frank—hailed the poem as a brilliant achievement. Later critical estimates have generally agreed with them by considering it Crane's first mature work. Philip Horton calls it "a milestone for him, marking the step from minor to major intention."[2]

The reason for this acclaim is clear. Crane had found an idiom that enabled him to present a universal theme in modern terms, and he had expressed an affirmative, hopeful point of view. The modern idiom represented a technical victory; his optimism was a personal triumph involving the employment of his talent in the service of idealism.

In sustaining contemporary imagery over more than 130 lines, Crane believed that he had at last found his own poetic voice. During the ten months of work on "Faustus and Helen," from April, 1922, until February, 1923, he had been tantalized by the power of modern details to evoke universal echoes. To capture this timeless element in timely imagery seemed the goal of all the arts. About music, he wrote, "Modern music almost drives me crazy! I went to hear D'Indy's *II Symphony* last night and my hair stood on end at its revelations. To get those, and others of men like Strauss, Ravel, Scriabin, and Bloch into *words,* one needs to *ransack* the vocabularies of Shakespeare, Jonson, Webster (for theirs were the richest) and add on scientific, street and counter, and psychological terms, etc. Yet I claim such things can be done!"[3] He felt that "Faustus and Helen" supported this claim. He was particularly pleased by the second section, which was the first to be written and was published separately as "The Springs of Guilty Song" in January, 1923. He considered it an articulation of the spirit and rhythm of jazz and as "something entirely new in English poetry."[4]

> Brazen hypnotics glitter here;
> Glee shifts from foot to foot,
> Magnetic to their tremolo.
> This crashing opéra bouffe,
> Blest excursion! this ricochet
> From roof to roof—

Throughout the entire poem he tried to select details imbued simultaneously with contemporary and universal significance. The "memoranda, baseball scores, the stenographic smiles and stock quotations" of the first section; the "metallic paradises" and "gyrating awnings" of the second, and the "corymbulous formations of mechanics" of the third—all were intended by their immediacy to engage the reader's responsiveness and to transport him to a timeless plane.

Crane hoped to use this modern idiom to support a positive idealistic theme. The strain of fear and unhappiness that has been remarked as recurrent in Crane's early poems suggests the personal effort that must have been necessary for him to assert such an affirmative view. In the early poems, modern conditions are found inimical to the most important human values: love, friendship, and art. Modernity is identified with vulgarity, materialism, and dehumanization. In the midst of these conditions spiritual satisfactions can at best be achieved only covertly and fleetingly. Where the wish for spiritual fulfillment is expressed, it is accompanied by the sad realization that it must be won in spite of the times. The poet commits himself to love in

"Chaplinesque," but his testimony is poignant because he foresees the defeat of his cause:

> We will sidestep, and to the final smirk
> Dally the doom of that inevitable thumb

Nonetheless, in "Faustus and Helen" Crane professes his faith
in the power of modern experience to sustain an idealistic
vision. He declares that intimations of beauty, love, and joy
exist in our times, but that men have lost the faculty of respond-
ing to them.

The encouragement to alter his outlook from despondence to
hopefulness came to Crane from several quarters. First, he found
the increasing pessimism of Eliot and his followers in the early
1920's unbearable. As they seemed to grow more despairing,
Crane cherished more highly his own affirmative experiences.
He knew both disappointments and satisfactions; the more
others saw only gloom, the more he felt obliged to speak up
for sunlight. As was noted earlier, he wrote at this time, "The
poetry of negation is beautiful—alas, too dangerously so for one
of my mind. But I am trying to break away from it. Perhaps
this is useless, perhaps it is silly—but one *does* have joys."[5]
Moreover, he had achieved some success in overcoming the
misery of his childhood. He had found his vocation—poetry,
and, although he had learned its demands, he had also known
its joys. The praise given his early work by several discerning
critics offset his being still generally unknown. Also, while
writing "Faustus and Helen," he had worked in advertising.
He had felt the conflict between commercial writing and
poetry, but he was pleased to be self-supporting.

In addition, he had become friendly with a group of creative
artists in Cleveland, and through them he had been made aware
of a growing desire among thoughtful people for a regeneration
of American culture. He began to draw strength from the efforts
of Van Wyck Brooks and other established writers like Lewis
Mumford, Waldo Frank, Sherwood Anderson, and Randolph
Bourne. These men were animated by the conviction that American culture was sterile and that its improvement depended upon
the cooperative labor of new intellectual and artistic leaders.

Their goal was to convert the nation from materialism to a more worthy ideal.

These cultural reformers accepted the analysis made by Brooks in his essays "America's Coming-of-Age," "Letters and Leadership," and "The Literary Life in America," (1915-1921) that "desiccated culture at one end and stark utility at the other have created a deadlock in the American mind, and all our life drifts chaotically between the two extremes."[6] They agreed also with his conclusion that America needed "an organized higher life."[7] It was to be led by young men—Young America, they called themselves— for the older generation had proved its incapacity. They were to rely upon the arts, especially literature, to extend their influence, "for poets and novelists and critics are the pathfinders of society."[8] In an essay on Randolph Bourne written many years later, Brooks expressed the common hope that had motivated these cultural rebels: "It was for a new fellowship in the youth of America as the principle of a great and revolutionary departure in our life, a league of youth, one might call it, consciously framed with the purpose of creating, out of the blind chaos of American society, a fine, free, articulate cultural order."[9]

A sense of fellowship and urgency was the most striking feature of this group. They believed that the success or failure of American civilization depended upon their efforts; their faith in themselves and their confidence in the attractiveness of their campaign to youth everywhere were intense. They were certain of their power and confident that they would use it for the improvement of the country. They believed, as Waldo Frank wrote, that "the soil stands ready to be turned."[10] Sherwood Anderson had written to Hart Crane of "the vague, intangible hunger to defeat the materialism of the world about. One hungers to find brothers buried away beneath all this roaring modern insanity of life. You in Akron, another man in California, a fellow . . . shivering in some cold room in New York."[11]

The keystone of this movement was its dedication to humanistic ideals. Waldo Frank, Crane's friend, extended this outlook to its most transcendental reaches by declaring that "we believe we are the true realists; we who insist that in the essence of all reality lies the Ideal"[12] and that "in this infancy of our adventure, America is a mystic Word. We go forth to seek

America."[13] However, Frank's fervid cultural Platonism was exceptional, and only Crane responded to it with genuine sympathy. Most of the group simply opposed materialism; in the tradition of humanism, they asserted the value of art, history, and the intellect. Lewis Mumford expressed the general view by writing that "idealism is a bad name for this mission; it is just as correct to call it realism; since it is part of the natural history of the human mind. What is valid in idealism is the belief in this process of re-molding, re-forming, re-creating, and so humanizing the rough chaos of existence."[14]

Crane wholeheartedly supported such a hopeful mission, and he dedicated his energies to its fulfillment. "I cry for a positive attitude!" he wrote in January, 1923.[15] A few days later he completed "Faustus and Helen." It celebrated his rejection of what he considered Eliot's negative influence. He explained that he intended his poem to assert a positive theme exactly opposite to the spirit of *The Waste Land,* which had appeared in 1922.

> I take Eliot as a point of departure toward an almost complete reverse of direction. . . . I would apply as much of his erudition and technique as I can absorb and assemble toward a more positive, or (if [I] must put it so in a sceptical age) ecstatic goal. . . . I feel that Eliot ignores certain spiritual events and possibilities as real and powerful now as, say, in the time of Blake.[16]

II *In Praise of Beauty*

The title "For the Marriage of Faustus and Helen" reveals the intention of the poem. It is to be affirmative—a song for a marriage. It is Crane's epithalamion to counter the blight of the sterile Waste Land. The marriage partners are to be Faustus—the aspiring man—and Helen—the paradigm of beauty, the fulfillment of man's quest for love. Unlike their chimerical union in *Doctor Faustus,* they are in Crane's poem to be joined in wedlock.

This ideal marriage is to take place in modern times. Critics have belabored the materialism—"the baked and labeled dough" —of the age; yet even amid routine duties and everyday distractions "smutty wings flash out equivocations." Although the skies are soot-laden, birds swing their bodies heavenward, and their ascensions quicken man's yearning. The evocative power of the birds occasions a grateful acknowledgment of their presence in the crowded city. Though "rebuffed by asphalt," they do not abandon city dwellers to their disheartening tasks but accompany them to work—"convoying divers dawn on every corner / To druggist, barber and tobacconist"—and, like them, the birds disappear in the evening.

> . . . to somewhere
> Virginal perhaps, less fragmentary, cool.

The departure of the birds at nightfall to lovelier places suggests that people, too, go off "somewhere" in the evening; they bear their workaday hours for the sake of private joys. Faustus recognizes with some wistfulness that there is *"the world dimensional"*—a place appropriate for the satisfaction of humble human needs—*"for those untwisted by the love of things irreconcilable."* But Faustus is not satisfied so simply. He seeks *"things irreconcilable,"* and he dedicates himself to the search for absolute beauty—for Helen. He has reflected upon the satisfactions of the ordinary life; now he affirms his faith in an ideal fulfillment. The setting for his declaration is significant. It is in the midst of a typically clangorous modern situation—a streetcar ride. Helen transcends time and awaits the tribute of love in all ages and circumstances. Though she is unseen by most men, Faustus may find her "eyes across an aisle, / Still flickering with those prefigurations—/ Prodigal."

In the fervor of his quickened belief in the possibility of meeting Helen—"There is some way, I think, to touch / Those hands of yours"—he pleads for the requital of his desire. He has bartered common satisfactions for a life of service to ideal beauty and love; he prays to be found worthy to receive their manifestations. As his supplication grows more intense, he praises all the ecstasies of life as reflections of Helen's beauty. Joys are intimations of her; grief symbolizes the distance between man's earthliness and her spirituality. Even the yearning men feel as they behold a clear sky is caused by its power to suggest her perfection.

Thinking of the earth lying distraught for the want of Helen suggests its physical destruction to Faustus. The legendary involvement of Helen with warfare, with "the press of troubled hands, too alternate / With steel and soil to hold you endlessly," enforces this reflection. The rubble of history challenges Faustus' idealism. He admits the challenge, but he reaffirms that his faith is superior even to the threat of physical annihilation. Helen is not endangered by war; her earthly captivity did not jeopardize her ideal freedom. She resides essentially on the timeless plane of beauty "beyond their million brittle, bloodshot eyes." There Faustus will meet her, not in any destructible earthly city but in "that world which comes to each of us alone." He is not to be frightened into abandoning his fealty to beauty because of the violence of the modern world. As Helen's postulant, he spurns both penitence and fear.

> The earth may glide diaphanous to death;
> But if I lift my arms it is to bend
> To you . . .

After rededicating himself to the search for beauty, even in the midst of global violence, Faustus humbly concludes his plea to Helen. He hesitates to ask for satisfaction; he requests only that his adoration be permitted. He prays that his solitary litany may be found acceptable:

> Accept a lone eye riveted to your plane,
> Bent axle of devotion along companion ways
> That beat, continuous, to hourless days—
> One inconspicuous, glowing orb of praise.

Crane's skill in this section in presenting an idealistic view in modern terms is apparent. Nevertheless, certain details are inadequate to his intention. First, it is the desire for marriage and not marriage itself that is celebrated. The title suggests fulfillment or at least union, but the text offers no indication of it. Faustus pledges himself to a quest for Helen; he prays for the requital of his search, but he does not experience it. This distinction between desire and fulfillment must be remembered in reading all of Crane's work. His hunger for the ideal was constant; its satisfaction was rarely, if ever, known. Second, the ability of this section to demonstrate the power of modern life to manifest ideal values, however fleetingly, is doubtful. Although Helen is found in a streetcar and the lives of city dwellers are viewed compassionately, there is little relationship between these facts and Faustus' faith. Men live in their "world dimensional" where Helen's eyes go "uncontested." Even the earth "may glide diaphanous to death." These conditions do not affect Faustus because he believes that Helen exists on a plane independent of the fate of the world. Although his faith was born amid modern circumstances, it has not been supported by modern life but seems rather to be held in its despite.

III *"The Springs of Guilty Song"*

The second section of "Faustus and Helen" was the first to be written, and it seemed sufficiently autonomous for Crane to submit it for separate publication. Entitled "The Springs of Guilty Song," it appeared in January, 1923. Crane thought of it as part of a longer poem of three sections, but he had not yet written the other two. After finishing this one he could say only that "the other parts are entirely unlike it, and God knows when they will be done."[17]

These facts about the composition of the second section suggest a possible incongruity between it and the others; the text confirms this surmise. The second section is a *tour de force* that stands in no closer than cousinly relationship to the rest of the poem. This kinship is the setting of the entire poem in modern times. In the first section Faustus discovered Helen in a streetcar; the second section is set in a roof-garden dance-hall because Crane wanted to present the sensual fulfillment of Faustus and Helen in a Dionysian revel. The first section was to celebrate ideal beauty and love; the second, to convey ecstasy. Unfortunately, the tone and attitude of the two sections are inharmonious. The first is reverential and meditative; the second, ironic and condescending. The sensual enjoyment described is not with the Helen of the first section to whom Faustus offered "one inconspicuous, glowing orb of praise" but with a silly flapper whom Faustus—a self-deprecating shadow of the aspiring protagonist of the first section—cannot forbear patronizing: "she is still so young, / We cannot frown upon her as she smiles." The name of Helen does not appear in this section, and the "marriage" described in it is a vulgar parody of the consummation anticipated in the first section.[18]

The root of the incongruity between the two sections is Crane's equivocal attitude toward modern times. He wanted to find epiphanies of his ideal within modern experience, but he could not. Indeed, he found modern behavior and idealism incompatible. As a result, he failed to maintain either the modern tone—as in the first section in which Helen resembles Aphrodite or the Virgin Mary more than a working girl—or his idealistic vision—as in the second.

Even though the second section fails to maintain the dramatic and thematic structure announced in the first, it has independent strength. A brilliant expression of the impact of the jazz age upon a shy, cultivated observer, it was the victory that Crane celebrated as "a work of youth and magic"[19] and it properly deserved to be published separately. In rhythm and imagery it conveys the compulsive tempo of a jazz band as a fascinated, nervous listener might hear it:

> Brazen hypnotics glitter here;
> Glee shifts from foot to foot,
>
> . . . .
>
> A thousand light shrugs balance us
> Through snarling hails of melody.
> White shadows slip across the floor
> Splayed like cards from a loose hand

The observer is startled by the self-abandonment of the dancers to the blaring music, but he resolves to "greet naively—yet intrepidly / New soothings, new amazements." Reluctant to express disapproval, he looks for some justification for the shrill revel. He decides that jazz offers release from the frightening realities of life. "This music has a reassuring way," he admits. The ecstasy of the dancers transforms a world terrified by "the groans of death" into a metallic paradise. Jazz offers a hysterical escape from the painfulness of life similar to the relief offered by the rituals of primitive religion.

After making this discovery, the observer cannot dismiss the young flapper—"the siren of the springs of guilty song"—

contemptuously. Her enticements are juvenile, but her impulse is universal. She seeks release and fulfillment. She joins the dance of life, although ignorant of its implications. Her ingenuousness conquers the observer's aloofness, and he tries to share with her the pleasing illusion of idyllic harmony:

> Let us take her on the incandescent wax
> Striated with nuances, nervosities
> That we are heir to: she is still so young,
> We cannot frown upon her as she smiles,
> Dipping here in this cultural storm
> Among slim skaters of the gardened skies.

IV *The Catharsis of War*

The third section of "Faustus and Helen" shifts from a concern for ideal beauty to a confrontation with the violence of modern warfare. This vision is anticipated in the first section when Faustus pledges devotion to Helen even though "the earth may glide diaphanous to death." There he feels that the collapse of the world would be a test of his dedication to beauty. Moreover, he is confident that he would triumph by ignoring all earthly throes and by remaining loyal to Helen, who dwells in a "world which comes to each of us alone." In the third section he no longer feels justified in ignoring the "rifts of torn and empty houses" and the "stubble streets." A world in agony is a test of his faith not only in beauty but in any kind of affirmation. Unless he can discover some bridge between the world he desires and the one he knows, his faith may be groundless.

He declares that the way to triumph over violence is to accept it. He admits terror and destruction, but he believes that from the experience of them the human spirit gains strength. Out of the acceptance of agony comes an increase in hopefulness. It is as though the experience of the worst assaults of matter demonstrates their limitations and encourages faith in the ability of the spirit to overcome them. Crane thought that this section provided a modern illustration of an ancient doctrine: "This last part begins with *catharsis*, the acceptance of tragedy through destruction (The Fall of Troy, etc. also in it). It is Dionysian in its attitude, the creator and the eternal destroyer dance arm in arm."[20] On the strength of this faith, Faustus can face the utmost carnage and still exclaim, "Let us unbind our throats of fear and pity."

Crane tries to convey the most vivid image of destruction, for, if the agony experienced is not total, an affirmation springing from it can not be totally convincing. Faustus, flying with an airman who has already carried out a combat mission, addresses his exhortation to him. He first refers to the pilot as a "capped arbiter of beauty" because of his awful power to destroy or preserve civilization. He then softens the impression of the pilot by calling him a "delicate ambassador / Of intricate slain numbers." The dexterous airman is not only a destroyer but a representative of the destroyed; he also "will fall too soon." He not only inflicts suffering but suffers himself. Knowing war on its most horrible terms, he is also to know its catharsis.

Faustus' next salutation to the pilot suggests the positive role of suffering. Faustus calls him a "religious gunman" and, farther on, an "eternal gunman." The pilot is placed in a priestly, even deific role at the same time that he is recognized as a destroyer. Because the ultimate triumph of man's spirit is in overcoming the destruction of matter, the pilot performs a liberating and religious function. Its affirmative—even joyful—character occasions Faustus' exclamation at the end of the first stanza: "Let us unbind our throats of fear and pity."

The following two stanzas demonstrate that Faustus' idealism—now attributed to the pilot as well—is based upon an awareness of the terror of life.

> We even,
> Who drove speediest destruction
> In corymbulous formations of mechanics,—
> Who hurried the hill breezes, spouting malice
> Plangent over meadows . . .
>
> .   .   .   .
>
> We know, external gunman, our flesh remembers
>
> .   .   .   .
>
> That saddled sky that shook down vertical
> Repeated play of fire—no hypogeum
> Of wave or rock was good against one hour.

Faustus has survived this holocaust, but he knows that, like all men, his tenure upon life is temporary. Before he also "curves to memory," he testifies to the spirituality of earthly existence.

First, Faustus asserts that man's joy in natural blessings encourages optimism. Recalling the abundance of prewar times, he declares that men shall always have "a goose, tobacco and cologne—/ Three-winged and gold-shod prophecies of heaven." These comforts, along with the "bells and voices" of society, are sufficient to outweigh the depressing deterioration of man's physical nature. The motive behind this reminder is not to foster a hedonistic naturalism but to encourage a wholesome natural outlook that will permit the signs of a higher destiny to be seen.

The next stanza—more crucial to the intention of this section—declares the positive value of suffering. Faustus states that agony is animated by the "voltage" of the spirit. From the heart of darkness, unexpected visions come of joyful fulfillment. Anchises and Erasmus experienced this transformation when, in the sea of their grief, they "gathered the voltage of blown blood and vine." Faustus urges his "brother-thief of time"—all mankind in the cycle of mortality—to plumb the core of suffering for presages of spiritual joy. "Delve upward for the new and scattered wine," he challenges. He repudiates the downcast spirit of those who cannot see beyond the horrors of the era. Suffering should not lead to dejection or to a craven obsession with guilt and remorse but to ecstasies. He curtly dismisses those who respond to contemporary tragedy by reviving religious sentiments of sin and punishment:

> Laugh out the meager penance of their days
> Who dare not share with us the breath released,
> The substance drilled and spent beyond repair
> For golden, or the shadow of gold hair.

Their flight is not forward toward joy through the ordeal of suffering but backward in fear toward the unworthy relief of self-abasement.

The poem ends as Faustus appeals for praise for the era which has been blamed and despaired of enough. Containing ineluctable encouragement to hopefulness, modern times deserve to be recognized as an opportunity for the spirit to triumph over suffering:

> Distinctly praise the years, whose volatile
> Blamed bleeding hands extend and thresh the height
> The imagination spans beyond despair,
> Outpacing bargain, vocable and prayer.

The exhortation of this section is the most fervid of the entire poem. Its support of positive ideal values is not remote as in the first section, nor tepid and ironic as in the second. It directly asserts the possibility of spiritual fulfillment within the violence of a war-torn age. It is Crane's retort to the tendency of his contemporaries to despair of civilization. As he had written in a letter: "Everyone, of course, wants to die as soon and as painlessly as possible! Now is the time for humor and the Dance of Death. All I know through very much suffering and dullness (somehow I seem to twinge more all the time) is that it interests me to still affirm certain things. That will be the persisting theme of the last part of 'F and H' as it has been all along."[21]

Nonetheless, the intensity of Crane's desire to "still affirm certain things" involved a liability. His utterances might seem shrill and vacuous to anyone lacking the personal experience to give them relevance. Crane could not express the fulfillment he championed because he had not known it. He believed in it, desired it, and exhorted others to do the same. To readers responsive to his desire, his fervor was galvanic; to the rest, it was brilliant bombast. The injunctions to optimism were splendid: "Let us unbind our throats of fear and pity," "share with us the breath released," and "distinctly praise the years," but the reasons for accepting them were obscure. At best he could offer a strong appeal to the will; he gave little help to the intellect.

This liability deserves emphasis because it is characteristic of all of Crane's poems that urge optimism and joy. The experience offered in the poem is generally weaker than the assertion made about it. Crane tried to make up for this weakness by the intensity of his will, by the sheer pressure of his desire for the fulfillment that he could not demonstrate. The truth is that Crane was neither a seer nor a mystic. His poems do not celebrate the triumph of idealism; their strength is in their eloquent expression of his yearning for such a triumph. His poems are songs of desire; at their best their fervor is irresistible.

However, sober reflection upon the distance between his

desire and its fulfillment was impossible for Crane following the completion of "Faustus and Helen." He rejoiced at having written his first long poem; he believed that he had realized both the modern diction and the idealistic theme that he had long sought. Moreover, his sense of victory was seconded by several critics. He wrote happily to Gorham Munson that Allen Tate had called him "the greatest contemporary American poet."[22] On the upsurge of this compliment, he felt himself "quite fit to become a suitable Pindar for the dawn of the machine age, so called. I have lost the last shreds of philosophical pessimism during the last few months. O yes, the 'background of life'—and all that is still there, but that is only three-dimensional. It is to the pulse of a greater dynamism that my work must revolve."[23] In the midst of his jubilation he was also planning a master poem that would justify these tributes to his talent. The same letters that celebrated the completion of "Faustus and Helen" announced his intentions for *The Bridge*.

CHAPTER 4

The Bridge

I *A Positive Vision of America*

THE CONNECTION is intimate between "For the Marriage of Faustus and Helen" and *The Bridge*. From the outset Crane announced *The Bridge* as an extension of the positive theme of the earlier poem. In February, 1923, he wrote to Gorham Munson: "I am ruminating on a new longish poem under the title of *The Bridge* which carries on further the tendencies manifest in 'F and H.'"[1] He no longer questioned his capacity to express an affirmative outlook; his new goal was to apply it to a much larger subject. The spiritual rebirth of the nation—the task assumed by many cultural reformers of the 1920's—provided exactly the scope he wanted. *The Bridge* was to make the same affirmation about American history that he believed "Faustus and Helen" had made about the contemporary scene. He made this link clear by telling Munson in February, 1923, that *The Bridge* "concerns a mystical synthesis of 'America.' History and fact, location, etc., all have to be . . . gathered up toward the climax of the bridge, symbol of our constructive future, our unique identity, in which is included also our scientific hopes and achievements of the future."[2]

To Crane, *The Bridge* was the proof and pinnacle of his career. From the completion of "Faustus and Helen" until the special edition of *The Bridge* by the Black Sun Press in January, 1930, he was dominated by this project. Although his productive periods during this time were unfortunately brief, the entire time was dedicated to *The Bridge;* all other compositions and activities were performed within its shadow. It exercised a seven-year fascination which shaped his poetic life, for he regarded work done before it as experimental and he wrote practically nothing after it. He never resisted its appeal, and he considered its difficulty a sign of its value. In 1926 he wrote to friends: "At times the project seems hopeless, horribly so; and then suddenly something happens inside one, and the theme and the substance of the conception seem brilliantly real, more so than ever! At least, *at worst,* the poem will be a *huge* failure!"[3]

II *Critical Reactions*

Crane's faith in *The Bridge* is justified by the poem itself and by the critical attention it has received. The poem satisfies the requirements for a major literary achievement. It has magnitude; in an age dominated by short poems, its length of more than 1,200 lines is impressive. It belongs with the few other important modern long poems: Eliot's *The Waste Land,* Pound's *The Cantos,* and Williams' *Paterson.* Moreover, its scope is commensurate with its length; perhaps it is even too vast. It encompasses the entire range of American experience; simultaneously, the history of America is used as an analogue to the growth of spiritual consciousness in the individual. The poem is intended as a synthesis of the past and as a projection into the future of the destiny of the individual and the nation.

The appearance of *The Bridge* was a major event in American letters. Judgments have been passed upon it ranging from the most adulatory—Henry Wells wrote that, "*The Bridge* is a noble and basically impersonal poem of epic vision fulfilling its author's boldest claims as a monument to America."[4]—to the opinions of Yvor Winters and Allen Tate that it had failed to realize its aim.[5] All, however, have indicated their awareness of the importance of the poem. Even negative reactions have acknowledged Crane's heroic endeavor and have attributed his failure in part to his excessive ambition. As he foresaw, where *The Bridge* is thought to have failed, it has failed hugely.

Tributes to *The Bridge* have been justified not only by Crane's intention but by his performance. Ultimate misgivings about the success of the poem have not prevented critics from recognizing that the writing in it is brilliant. In his important essay "Hart Crane" Allen Tate states that the poem contains lyrics "the best of which are not surpassed by anything in American literature."[6] Reserving the right to differ about which sections are the best,

other critics have agreed with him. It is now generally granted
that *The Bridge* has a rhetorical intensity and imaginative sweep
matched in American literature only by Whitman.

A poem as ambitious and complex as *The Bridge* needs to be
approached carefully. First, it is noteworthy that several of the
earliest reviewers criticized it on the basis of a false expectation;
it was scored for not being what an unprejudiced reader never
expects it to be.[7] Ironically, the principal source of confusion was
Crane himself. He caused it by his effusiveness. He discussed his
work in progress with his friends and released sections for publication as soon as they were written. The published sections
aroused curiosity about the entire scheme, and he usually
answered inquiries in superlatives. Also, in December, 1925, he
received a grant from Otto Kahn, a patron of the arts, to give him
leisure to finish the poem. His request and his subsequent progress reports were appropriately grandiloquent, and they increased the expectations of what he was about.

By far the most unfortunate remark made by Crane was that
he was writing an epic. Related to this claim, and only slightly
less damaging, was the announcement that *The Bridge* was the
expression of a cultural myth. These claims aroused expectations
that led later to complaints that the poem did not live up to them.
There was considerable justification for such criticism. Crane had
created these expectations, and he could not blame others for
asking him to meet them.

When the concept of *The Bridge* was first quickening his
imagination, Crane announced to Gorham Munson that the poem
would be a "mystical synthesis" of America that would gather the
significance of the nation's past and present into a symbolic projection of its glorious future. He added that he was "grateful for
your very rich suggestions best stated in your *Frank Study* [a
criticism of the work of Waldo Frank] on the treatment of
mechanical manifestations of today as subject for lyrical, dramatic,
and even epic poetry."[8] He soon realized that the grand scheme
he contemplated could be handled only in a poem of major
dimensions. In his first letter to Otto Kahn, he described the
intention of *The Bridge* as the enumeration of "a new cultural
synthesis of values in terms of our America."[9] From this time on
he continually associated its content with myth and its form with

the epic. In August, 1926, he wrote to Frank of his joy at handling "the beautiful skeins of this myth of America."[10] A year later he reported triumphantly to his patron, "What I am really handling, you see, is the Myth of America."[11] In the same letter he explicitly related his poem to the classical epic. In a plea for continued support on the basis of the magnificent design of his poem, he wrote: "*The Aeneid* was not written in two years—nor in four, and in more than one sense I feel justified in comparing the historic and cultural scope of *The Bridge* to this great work. It is at least a symphony with an epic theme, and a work of considerable profundity and inspiration."[12]

Unfortunately these statements were radically misleading, and they have hindered the proper consideration of the poem. Crane was not writing an epic nor a myth because he was not writing a narrative poem. *The Bridge* contained elements that might be employed in an epic or myth, but it lacked the central prerequisite that they be bound coherently in narration. Crane possessed neither the equipment nor the impulse to dramatize the history of America. His poetic sensibility was personal, and he recognized this fact in his admission to Allen Tate following the publication of *The Bridge*: "My vision of poetry *is* too personal to 'answer the call.'"[13] The pity is that he ever believed or suggested that it was otherwise, for the truth is, as Yvor Winters aptly remarked, that "*The Bridge* is a loosely joined sequence of lyrics."[14]

Crane was led to foster this misapprehension by his enthusiasm and his carelessness. He believed that his project was magnificent; accordingly he strained to find descriptive terms adequate to his faith. With regrettable imprecision he appropriated those of "epic" and "myth." To him the first signified a subject of heroic proportions; the second, the spiritual motivation with which he approached it. He chose them because they seemed honorific and commensurate to the noble task he had assumed.

III *Crane's Intentions*

It is noteworthy also that the false expectations caused by Crane's use of these terms might have been avoided if other remarks that he made about *The Bridge* had been as strictly heeded. His candor caused some confusion but also resulted in several clarifying observations. They indicate what he actually meant by "epic" and "myth" and what he hoped the poem would be.

First, Crane clearly established that he planned *The Bridge* as a sequel to "For the Marriage of Faustus and Helen"—as another witness to the contemporary possibilities of idealism. Despite the materialism and violence of modern culture, Faustus declared his faith in man's capacity to penetrate beyond the "world dimensional" to a plane of absolute values. He even claimed that intimations of this plane were present in the ordinary details of contemporary life—trolley cars, street corners, and dance halls. He found that amid city life "smutty wings flash out equivocations," and he dedicated himself to the ever-present absolutes of beauty and love.

The Bridge was to declare the same faith. In subway trains and burlesque houses and on Wall Street, ocean liners, and old Connecticut estates, the poet was to testify to his belief in "some Word that will not die." Support for this faith was to be found in the record of the past, but fundamentally *The Bridge* was to present an idealistic view of modern times.

The bond between "Faustus and Helen" and *The Bridge* is indicated further by Crane's explicit view of the second poem as a more forceful counterthrust to Eliot's *The Waste Land* than the earlier had been. He felt that only a poem of the proportions of *The Waste Land* could overcome its debilitating influence. He saw Eliot's work as a challenge: "In a way it's a test of materials as much as a test of one's imagination. *Is* the last statement sentimentally made by Eliot,

> This is the way the world ends,
> This is the way the world ends,—
> Not with a bang but a whimper.

is this acceptable or not as the poetic determinism of our age?!"[15] Later, following the publication of *The Bridge,* he explained how Eliot's poem had affected his intention: "The poem, as a whole, is, I think, an affirmation of experience, and to that extent is 'positive' rather than 'negative' in the sense that *The Waste Land* is negative."[16]

The second important explanation provided by Crane about

The Bridge concerns his use of the past. While he felt that he had been successful in "Faustus and Helen," he believed that a still stronger case could be made for his position. He was convinced that, in addition to the encouragements to idealism that he recognized in modern times, the entire history of America supported his faith. Consequently, he decided to extend the range of his new poem in order to enhance the persuasiveness of his theme. Instances of idealism and of events that supported faith in it from the past would be used to bolster the faith of modern readers. These affirmative experiences of the past would help overcome the pressure of contemporary negativism. Crane's faith did not depend upon the past; it was founded on personal grounds, not on history, but he recognized that its attractiveness could be increased by evidence from earlier times. He explained to Otto Kahn in 1927: "What I am after is an assimilation of this experience [the history of America], a more organic panorama, showing the continuous and living evidence of the past in the inmost vital substance of the present."[17] He sought to present a series of past events charged with idealistic overtones that would quicken the reader's responsiveness to similar ones in the present.

The difference between the poem Crane planned and an epic is clear. He did not intend to offer a coherent narration of any portion of American history. He did not intend to equate a particular theme with our national experience. Nor did he rely upon his use of the past to prove his theme. He wished to support faith in idealism amid modern conditions by demonstrating its viability at several junctures of the American past. The role of the past was to be persuasive because of the reader's sympathy with the history of his country. Crane did not claim that idealism had characterized our past, simply that grounds for idealism could be discovered there. Naturally, the more crucial the instances, the more effectively they would serve his interest, but he never felt obliged to justify his selections historically, Success was to depend more upon his lyrical than upon his historical skill.

Crane's use of the past resembled Eliot's in *The Waste Land*. Both were eclectic, choosing references from many sources to support their theme. Eliot drew upon diverse cultures, and his far-flung reach probably prevented anyone from thinking that he had attempted an epic. Crane confined himself to America and thereby encouraged expectations for a national epic.

IV *Support from America's "Usable Past"*

As was mentioned earlier, Crane's endeavor to repudiate materialism by presenting examples of idealism in American history bound him to the movement in the 1920's that aimed at the cultural rebirth of the nation. It is his point of contact with men like Waldo Frank, Van Wyck Brooks, and Lewis Mumford. Like them, he dismissed materialism as unworthy of America, and he believed he had found in American history many traces of a higher spirit. These traces constituted the "Usable Past" and were to set in motion a new wave of the future. Significantly, the features of the past that these reformers found most evocative were practically the same ones used by Crane in *The Bridge*: Columbus' discovery, the destiny of the Indian, the frontiersman, the seafarer, the mechanical feats of modern times—especially the airplane, the Brooklyn Bridge, and the Woolworth Building—and the literary artists of the American nineteenth-century renaissance.

Crane's explicit reference in *The Bridge* to the great nineteenth-century American writers—Poe, Melville, Whitman, and Emily Dickinson—points to a cardinal feature of American literature. He found support for his idealism among the major writers of our tradition. He discovered that, although materialism has generally dominated our popular culture, idealism has held a central place in our "classic" literature. As Charles Feidelson, Jr., has shown in his *Symbolism and American Literature*, the recognition of both the spiritual essence of matter and the power of symbols to communicate this inner life of things is a constant feature of American literature. It has been present in varying degrees of strength from Puritan times to the present, and it is the unifying element in the work of the nineteenth-century masters.[18] Next to Crane's personal intuition, his greatest strength was the knowledge that this theme placed him in such company.

The influence of these writers on *The Bridge* is unmistakable. From Poe and Whitman, Crane received encouragement to his faith in the vatic power of the poet. They—and behind Whitman stands the shaping vision of Emerson's "The Poet"—insisted that true poetry presents insights into the eternal order of things. It is a fleeting fulfillment of man's perennial desire to overcome temporal limitations. In the Preface to *Leaves of Grass,* Whitman declared that the poet "sees eternity in men and women." In "The Poetic Principle," Poe—using terms strikingly like Crane's statements about his own artistic intentions—explained the transcendental function of poetry:

> We have still a thirst unquenchable. . . . This thirst belongs to the immortality of Man. It is at once a consequence and an indication of his perennial existence. It is the desire of the moth for the star. It is no mere appreciation of the Beauty before us—but a wild effort to reach the Beauty above. Inspired by an ecstatic prescience of the glories beyond the grave, we struggle by multiform combinations among the things and thoughts of Time, to attain a portion of that loveliness whose very elements, perhaps, appertain to eternity alone. And thus when by Poetry . . . we find ourselves melted into tears—we weep them . . . through a certain, petulant, impatient sorrow at our inability to grasp *now,* wholly, here on earth, at once and for ever, those divine and rapturous joys, of which *through* the poem . . . we attain to but brief and indeterminate glimpses.[19]

In the writings of Emily Dickinson and Herman Melville, Crane found corroboration of his belief that the world contains traces of the ideal for those who have eyes to see. Emily Dickinson had written:

> This world is not conclusion;
>   A sequel stands beyond,
> Invisible, as music,
>   But positive, as sound.
> It beckons and it baffles;
>   Philosophies don't know,
> And through a riddle, at the last,
>   Sagacity must go.[20]

Crane was dedicated to the pursuit of these beckonings that elude the rigors of philosophy but condescend to the submission of a poet. From Melville no particular text need be cited to show the kinship between Crane and the introspective mariner. All of *Moby Dick* asserts the presence of metaphysical values in matter. "Strike through the mask!" cried Captain Ahab, in explaining to the astonished Starbuck that a whale is not just a bulk but an embodiment of spirit. Crane accepted this explanation fully, for it was his strongest conviction. He missed, however, the warning in Captain Ahab's fate that the spirit may be inscrutable or evil as well as good and that identifying oneself with it may be self-destructive as well as fulfilling. Crane believed with Melville that spirit informed matter, but he was too close to the hopefulness of Emerson and Whitman to doubt that the nature of this spirit could be anything but benign. It is interesting to wonder if Crane ever read *Pierre;* for, like Pierre, he struggled to live according to chronological (celestial) time rather than by horological (terrestial) standards. And to him, as to Pierre, Melville's solemn warning was appropriate: "Almost invariably, with inferior beings, the absolute effort to live in this world according to the strict letter of the chronometricals is, somehow, apt to involve those inferior beings eventually in strange *unique* follies and sins, unimagined before."[21]

In conclusion, *The Bridge* should be read as an exhortation to idealism rather than a demonstration of it. It provides illustrations from the American past in order to encourage faith in the present and the future. It is not an epic but a series of lyrics intended to quicken an affirmative, idealistic viewpoint. Its success depends upon the relationship between its general theme and the particular ways Crane attempts to encourage the reader to accept it. Whether the individual sections depend upon a prior commitment to idealism, or persuade to this belief, or discourage one from it, must be closely observed.

V *Explication of The Bridge*

Both the structure of the poem and its leading symbol are indicated by the title. Literally it refers to the Brooklyn Bridge, considered by Crane the most beautiful bridge in the world and a symbol of the finest employment of modern ingenuity. He lived near the bridge for years and never lost his reverence for its design. It seemed a holy thing to him, uplifting to the spirit and evocative of the passage he sought from time to eternity. In its function as a span between two shores, it represented his intention in the poem of making connections between the present and the past and of moving rapidly from one historical episode to another.

Proem: "To Brooklyn Bridge"

The introductory poem, "To Brooklyn Bridge," celebrates the bridge as a symbol. At the outset it is recognized as a representation of man's desire to transcend ordinary experience, to win spiritual fulfillment. It is then addressed as a demigod capable of aiding men in their quest because of the spiritual energy and insight implicit in its design.

The premise of the poem is that all men desire spiritual exaltation. Man's pursuit of the eternal plane may be obscured and disguised, but behind every expression of human striving is dissatisfaction with the conditions of time and a yearning for permanence and purity. This need enables the sight of seagulls "shedding white wings of tumult, building high / Over the chained bay waters Liberty—" to lift man's spirit from its mundane slavery to visions of unfettered freedom. So, too, does it explain man's incessant search for an epiphany, a sign, of his higher fulfillment. The "multitudes bent toward some flashing scene" at the movies are looking for a vision that "panoramic sleights" cannot provide but which they continue to seek with undying hope.

This need also prompts veneration of the bridge, for, unlike movies and gulls, this human contrivance has undergone an apotheosis because of the purity and beauty that have been embodied in its structure.

> And Thee, across the harbor, silver-paced
> As though the sun took step of thee, yet left
> Some motion ever unspent in thy stride,—
> Implicitly thy freedom staying thee!

Standing amid the tensions of the modern city, the bridge offers its "vibrant reprieve and pardon" from disorder and uplifts the aspirations of desperate wayfarers. Animated by purer energies than the communities it joins, the bridge has transcended commerce to become a "harp and altar," a sublime realization that leads toward the fulfillment "of the prophet's pledge, / Prayer of pariah, and the lover's cry." In it, through the creative power of its builders, the most solid and durable of the earth's elements have been fused in "unfractioned idiom" to "condense eternity."

The poet's reverence for the bridge because of its power to awaken and affirm his idealism impels him to pray to it. Its transformation from matter to an incarnation of the ideal is then complete. It may be invoked as well as respected. In language reserved usually for supplicating the Almighty—or, in Christian worship, Christ, the mediator between God and man—the poet confesses his need and beseeches assistance:

> O Sleepless as the river under thee,
> Vaulting the sea, the prairies' dreaming sod,
> Unto us, lowliest sometime sweep, descend
> And of the curveship lend a myth to God.

Thus the proem clearly announces the intention of the entire poem. Man's need for an idealistic faith and the power of the bridge to aid in its achievement are acknowledged. The bridge is honored as a span between time and the timeless. So perfectly does the Brooklyn Bridge symbolize this function and so alluring are its incitements, that the poet is impelled to search within its glow for further support of his belief. From its towers he sees earlier spans across the American past, anticipations of this climactic expression. He trusts that the cumulative strength of these many bridges will constitute a sure "myth to God."

"Ave Maria"

From the invocation to the Brooklyn Bridge as a symbol of America's link with her spiritual future, a transition is made to the birth of the nation. Here, too, the poet finds a spanning of the unknown sustained by courage and faith—Columbus' voyage of discovery. Thus in one great thrust the extremes of the American experience are bridged, and it is claimed that each terminus is itself a bridge to the Absolute. Columbus' journey was from the Old World to the alluring possibility of the New. The principal motive of his journey was spiritual. Deeper than the desire for riches was his hope for higher human experiences, for a fresh and pure start for the human spirit. Courage to sustain this endeavor was drawn from his faith in God's support.

In this section, a dramatic monologue, Columbus has already discovered America and is bound for Spain to report his success. A storm rages, and he fears that he may die before his achievement is known. He prays for help and reflects upon his experience. He understands the significance of his discovery. He has found Cathay; despite the scepticism of critics, he has reached "the Chan's great continent." "Chan" here suggests God and "Cathay" the land of fulfillment. Out of the bitter test of "bewilderment and mutiny," "tempest-lash and surfeitings," he has been victorious. He prays now for the safe return of at least one ship so that others may learn of his victory and share in its virtue.

Columbus recognizes that his achievement has primarily been spiritual and that it has been made possible by faith. "Cathay" is a place; but, more important, it is also a new opportunity for the human spirit. It will yield its riches to love, not to greed. Knowing well the greed of his patrons, he cries out in warning:

> —Yet no delirium of jewels! O Fernando,
> Take of that eastern shore, this western sea,
> Yet yield thy God's, thy Virgin's charity!

> —Rush down the plenitude, and you shall see
> Isaiah counting famine on this lee!

The courage of Columbus to pursue his dream has come from faith in its righteousness and in Divine Providence. On the night before sighting land, it was "faith, not fear / Nigh surged me witless," he recalls. His faith stood the test of an uncharted ocean crossing. For this victory a difficult combination of confidence and humility was demanded: confidence, to overcome doubt; humility, to submit entirely to the will of God. The poem ends with the assertion that human events are governed by God and that spiritual progress depends upon man's acceptance of severe self-discipline.

The monologue at sea concludes with Columbus' realization that his prayer for a safe return has been granted. The setting then changes to the royal court where Columbus offers a *Te Deum* of thanksgiving to God. Its burden is the paradox of divine love, for, although man seeks spiritual goals as the only true fulfillment of his nature, he resists the pain that their pursuit involves. Consequently, he must be compelled to pursue what alone can satisfy him.

God is praised for searching "cruelly with love thy parable of man." The divine Wisdom simultaneously tests and guides His fortunate victims, leading them on a course of self-abnegation toward self-fulfillment in Him. Columbus recognizes that this course is the inner meaning of all journeys into the unknown. He sees that in being prompted toward Cathay he was being drawn always toward "still one shore beyond desire" and that the value of the New World lies in its physical manifestation of a spiritual goal. He thanks God for driving him to this insight.

> Te Deum laudamus
> O Thou Hand of Fire

Columbus has discovered the meaning of America. With the vision of faith he sees that the route he has traced from the Old World to the New is a symbol of the passage of the soul to God. America's brightest destiny will be to maintain the radiance of a spiritual Cathay.

"Powhatan's Daughter"

The passage of Columbus to the New World was presented in "Ave Maria" as an analogue of the ascension of the spirit from time to eternity. America, the end of the journey, had the effulgence of a heavenly kingdom. Next, the history of the continent is explored for experiences that can sustain and foster this sacramental character. Whereas "Ave Maria" celebrated the first bridge to America, "Powhatan's Daughter" celebrates bridges launched from native soil. As Crane explained to Otto Kahn, "Powhatan's daughter, or Pocahontas, is the mythological nature-symbol chosen to represent the physical body of the continent, or the soil. . . . The five sub-sections of Part II are mainly concerned with a gradual exploration of this 'body' whose first possessor was the Indian."[22] These sub-sections are "The Harbor Dawn," "Van Winkle," "The River," "The Dance," and "Indiana."

The transition in time from "Ave Maria" to "The Harbor Dawn" is abrupt. Pleased to discover "that a bridge is begun from the two ends at once,"[23] Crane located this section in the present. In setting, however, it follows easily after the voyage of Columbus. The scene is the New York harbor "400 years and more" later. The virginal soil that Columbus warned must be turned with love has been assaulted by industry:

> And then a truck will lumber past the wharves
> As winch engines begin throbbing on some deck;
> Or a drunken stevedore's howl and thud below
> Comes echoing alley-upward through dim snow.

Only in sleep is the pure and fertile promise of the soil still felt in its primal urgency. In modern times dreams are needed to fortify the spirit against the onslaught of daily affairs. The poet awakens reluctantly to the insistent reveille of commerce. Columbus awaited the dawn eagerly and found his faith justified, but the modern seeker knows that urban life opposes idealism. He is grateful to the "soft sleeves of sound" that "attend the darkling harbor, the pillowed bay," for water is proof against the materialism of the land. He cherishes the reprieve offered by the soft harbor sounds to dream of the fulfillment of his search for a loving relationship with the continent. He imagines that Pocahontas—the virgin soil of Amerca—lies beside him, receptive to his seed.

> *your hands within my hands are deeds;*
> *my tongue upon your throat—singing*
> *arms close; eyes wide, undoubtful*
> > *dark*
> > > *drink the dawn—*
> *a forest shudders in your hair!*

Bearing the memory of this vision, the poet faces the reality of city-life. "Cyclopean towers across Manhattan waters" become visible and call him to his tasks. His challenge is to remain true to his spiritual aim in the midst of a hubbub.

In "Van Winkle," the next poem, the poet sets about the business of the day. His conflict is no longer between dreams and reality; it is between the constraint of adulthood and the freer, more exciting time of his youth. This contrast is extended, by means of the poet's recollections, to the earliest and most

recent years of the country's history. He establishes a link
between his personal experience and the nation's that is fundamental to the structure of the poem. The poet's day from dawn
to evening is analogous to the history of the country from its
discovery to the present. In "Van Winkle" the poet on his way
to work recalls the adventurous hopes of his boyhood in images
of the early explorers and settlers he once read about in school.
Pizarro, Cortez, Priscilla, Captain John Smith, and Rip Van
Winkle were his companions then, in a time of excitement and
promise. Now the limitless opportunities of America have been
channeled into a mainstream of commerce. Down all the high-
ways from Far Rockaway to the Golden Gate, people meekly
hurry to work. The leisurely society that harbored Rip Van
Winkle has succumbed to the rigorous demands of business.
Sadly the poet reflects that *Van Winkle sweeps a tenement
/ Way down on Avenue A."* In Van Winkle's fate he foresees his
own—"And hurry along, Van Winkle—it's getting late!"

The poet also recalls certain incidents from his childhood
that bear only indirectly upon the American experience, but
these are important in accounting for his spiritual hunger. He
remembers being punished and rejected by his parents:

> Is it the whip stripped from the lilac tree
> One day in spring my father took to me,
> Or is it the Sabbatical, unconscious smile
> My mother almost brought me once from church
> And once only, as I recall—?

These experiences are the negative counterparts to the positive
incitements of youth's dreams. Their pain goads the poet toward
some fulfillment in which grief will be unknown. It is toward
this goal that he struggles as he hurries to the subway.

"The River," a section generally considered one of the most
successful of *The Bridge,* is vital in establishing the theme of the
entire poem. It demonstrates three facets of Crane's idealism:
two are in keeping with the announced intention of the poem;
one, disturbingly at odds with it. The two congruous ones are
that the land exerts a unifying spiritual influence upon those
who live upon it and that there is widespread blindness to this

influence in modern times. The third is the suspicion that human experience contributes only to a meaningless flow of time.

The first two convictions are introduced simultaneously by an extension of the action that ended "Van Winkle." Van Winkle was hurrying to catch his train; in "The River" his conveyance has been transformed into the Twentieth Century Limited racing across the continent. Its high speed affords a kaleidoscopic view of a superficial and confused culture. All the features of modern life pass the train in pell-mell chaos. The mundane and the sublime are jumbled beyond distinction: "SCIENCE— COMMERCE and the HOLYGHOST." No profound experience is possible in a society in which nerves are kept at hysterical pitch by an incessant nightmare of noise, motion, and color. This condition is especially pernicious because it is exactly what people think they want: "Breathtaking—as you like it . . . eh?" Having based their dreams upon speed and convenience, they cannot recognize the "telegraphic night" to which they have doomed themselves.

Ironically, the only ones to escape the catalepsy of modern society are its failures. Those who cannot adjust to the pace of the Twentieth Century Limited have a chance to keep in touch with deeper currents. Their failure to be up-to-the-minute may mean their success in preserving a vision of eternity. In keeping with the image in which the transcontinental railroad symbolizes modern society, these fortunate failures are the hoboes:

> Three men, still hungry on the tracks, ploddingly
> Watching the tail lights wizen and converge, slip-
> ping gimleted and neatly out of sight.

These men, born out of time, are holdovers from an earlier, slower epoch. In a world of "keen instruments, strung to a vast precision," they live by more primal guides. The slow seasons changing the face of the land are their time schedules. They move in apparent aimlessness yet with deep instinctive wonder and love for the mystery of the country.

Crane's tender elegiac presentation of the homeless wanderers is charged with the awareness of both their pathos and their triumph. As a man and poet he feels akin to their forlorn fate;

yet he is sufficiently detached to see them squarely: "I have trod the rumorous midnights, too." He recognizes the personal shortcomings that have led to and been intensified by their ostracism from society:

> The ancient men—wifeless or runaway
> Hobo-trekkers that forever search
> An empire wilderness of freight and rails.
> Each seemed a child, like me, on a loose perch,
> Holding to childhood like some termless play.

He also sees that the failure to establish a place in society throws the hoboes back upon the land. In a more completely dependent way than city-dwellers can realize, these drifters rely upon the continent for strength. They need the land, and their necessity makes them sensitive to its intimations. "Yet they touch something like a key perhaps. / From pole to pole across the hills, the states / —They know a body under the wide rain." This knowledge, their triumph, places them in sympathy with nature's deepest meaning.

This meaning is the third important perception of "The River," but it is also the one that casts a shadow upon the idealistic theme of *The Bridge*. The meaning of the body of America—so intimately known to the hoboes and to the people of earlier generations—is the ultimate immersion of everything in the flux of time. It is symbolized in the title, "The River," which in America is the Mississippi. In its waters all the experience of America is united, "for you, too, feed the River timelessly." Distinctions and separations, factions and foes are joined as "grimed tributaries to an ancient flow." In its unqualified acceptance and fusion of the "damp tonnage and alluvial march of days," the river is nature's egalitarian instrument in effecting brotherhood.

However, this leveling phenomenon is interpreted in a way counter to the theme of the poem. According to the theme, man's goal is his conscious spiritual participation in the ideal; "The River" suggests that individuals have no further end than to join the indiscriminate passage of all things in time. Swollen with the mass of creation, the river is "tortured with history, its one will—flow!" The theme points to the overcoming of

time in eternity; "The River" offers only annihilation in time's
inevitable and inscrutable movement. The direction of idealism is
upward; the inescapable movement of "The River" is downward:

> —The Passion spreads in wide tongues, choked and slow,
> Meeting the Gulf, hosannas silently below.

"The Dance," the fourth section of "Powhatan's Daughter,"
evokes a time when the land was foremost in the consciousness
of those who lived upon it. It celebrates the nature rituals of
the Indians, who knew the continent as a lover his beloved.
It contrasts them with modern Americans who reject the land
for machinery. The transition to this earlier era was begun
in "The River." The poet, in sympathy with the wandering
derelicts, had recalled that long ago "papooses crying on the
wind's long mane / Screamed redskin dynasties that fled the
brain, / —Dead echoes!" This contact with the past is fulfilled
in "The Dance" by means of his imaginative participation in an
Indian fertility ritual.

The relationship of the Indian to the land is expressed in
erotic imagery. Pocahontas, the "Princess whose brown lap was
virgin May; / And bridal flanks and eyes hid tawny pride,"
is the fecund, life-giving soil of the continent. The Indian is
her lover—here represented by Maquokeeta, a Sachem. His
passion is dramatized in the steps of a dance; its climax is his
death, and its fulfillment is his transfiguration. Dying in an
ecstasy of love, he wins immortality as a spirit watching eternally
over the land:

> Thewed of the levin, thunder-shod and lean,
> Lo, through what infinite seasons dost thou gaze—
> Across what bivouacs of thin angered slain,
> And see'st thy bride immortal in the maize!

The poet attempts to associate himself with this ritual. He
values the spiritualization of natural life achieved by the Indian
and regrets its loss in modern times. He yearns to participate in
the primitive drama but realizes that he is remote from the
Indian. The reason is twofold: the hostility between the races
and his own alienation from nature. The white man invaded the

soil of the Indian; the Indian withdrew to shield Pocahontas from the enemies' advances. "Greeting they sped us, on the arrow's oath: / Now lie incorrigibly what years between." Consequently, the white man has never established a loving and ennobling bond either with nature or with the Indian. To do so, he would have to undergo an initiation that would acquaint him with the spiritual energies of the land.

The poet imagines himself experiencing such an initiation. He is required to journey away from the modern life of the settlements to the more natural way of the Indians. He is willing—"I left the village for dogwood"—and begins the work of personal regeneration. As he discards the baggage of his old life, he enjoys new intimacies with nature. At last he reaches his goal, "grey tepees tufting the blue knolls ahead, / Smoke swirling through the yellow chestnut glade." As he yields to the appeal of Indian life, he is purged of the white man's prejudices—"its rhythm drew, / —Siphoned the black pool from the heart's hot root!"—and he becomes capable of sharing in the Indians' vital communion with nature.

He then witnesses a ritual dance of death and transformation performed by Maquokeeta. He understands the motivation of the Indian's total surrender to nature and encourages him to it. Death will liberate Maquokeeta from time and ensure his freedom in eternity. He will be like the "snake that lives before, / That casts his pelt, and lives beyond!" The poet tries desperately to identify himself with the Indian, but he fails. In an outcry of frustrated desire, he admits his fundamental alienation from the myth he has been celebrating:

> . . . Medicine-man, relent, restore—
> Lie to us,—dance us back the tribal morn!

Having admitted his failure, he expresses his joyfulness over the Indian's success. He praises the ritual as though convinced of its validity. His final vision is of the Indian transfigured in the glory of his triumph:

> Like one white meteor, sacrosanct and blent
> At last with all that's consummate and free
> There, where the first and last gods keep thy tent.

The concluding section of "The Dance" is an ode to the continent, the "bride immortal in the maize." The beauty and fecundity of the land suggest freedom and fulfillment to those whose nature has not been corrupted by superficial lures:

> West, west and south! winds over Cumberland
> And winds across the llano grass resume
> Her hair's warm sibilance. Her breasts are fanned
> O stream by slope and vineyard—into bloom!

Before such wholesome and heaven-scented abundance the poet momentarily feels as transfigured as the Indian Prince. They are fraternally united in the spirit that dwells in the land they love. Together they have overcome the distraction of society and in "cobalt desert closures made our vows." The poet's effort to remain faithful to his dedication in the present is inspired by the example of the Indian in the past.

"Indiana," the final tribute to the land in "Powhatan's Daughter," is weak. It is intended to serve as a transition to the next section, "Cutty Sark," but the difficulty of establishing a line of kinship from the Indians to the white settlers of the prairie states, and from them to the sailors of the Yankee clipper ships is too great. The pace is hurried, and the intensity of presentation—so remarkable in the preceding sections—falls off badly. The reader is not surprised to learn that its composition gave Crane trouble and that it was finished hastily just before *The Bridge* went to press.

His purpose was to demonstrate that the white settlers inherited the Indians' spiritual relationship to the soil and, in turn, extended it to the sea. A mother tells her son, who is leaving to follow the sea, of the loving relationship with the land that an Indian squaw bequeathed to her when they met on the plains years before. The squaw, dispossessed of the land, was journeying westward; the white woman, defeated in the search for gold in California, was traveling east to settle in former Indian territory. Each carried a son, and, as they passed, the Indian silently granted the land to the white child. Now the land has been cultivated, and the grown son is going to sea. His mother urges him to establish there the same bond of love that has supported them on land. Unfortunately, the mother's exhortation is trite; as a result, the thematic significance of the poem is blurred.

"Cutty Sark"

The sea is the next phase of American experience to be presented. The approach is contemporary. The poet meets an old drunken sailor in a South Street bar. The sailor—he may be the same man who leaves for the sea in "Indiana"—reminisces about his adventures. His disjointed remarks are interwoven with a song played on a pianola as well as with the poet's narration of the incident. Altogether these elements form a medley that evokes the beauty and mystery of the sea and the exhilaration of life on clipper and whaling ships.

The terrors of the sea have ruined the old sailor for life on land. "Murmurs of Leviathan he spoke," and, like Melville's sailors, he expresses awe at having encountered some mysterious spirit in nature. The intensity of his experience has broken him. Only alcohol can arouse the fearsome visions that continue to fascinate him; so, "rum was Plato in our heads."

The old sailor is obsessed by time: "I'm not much good at time any more," he admits, and then argues with himself about what he has said. He insists that he really does know "what time it is" and then protests that he does not want to know. The conflict remains unsettled, but he indicates its cause: "that / damned white Arctic ruined my time." His quandary is that he has become aware of the mingling of time and eternity. Most men are aware only of time; they are limited in understanding but undisturbed. Those who gain knowledge of timelessness are few; what they learn overwhelms them by its amplitude and cripples them by its inaccessibility. They must live with the memory of what they can seldom realize. Having encountered something that exposed the limits of time—in the sailor's case, the frozen whiteness at the Arctic—they have met reality on a level that most men do not even know to exist.

As the sailor speaks, hints of cities long submerged beneath the sea—places of fulfillment in the past or future—are heard in the song played on the pianola. They express another aspect of the sea's fascination. Despite man's customary preference for the land, his thoughts turn to the sea when his imagination leaps beyond his own brief life to eternity. The sailor has touched eternity and has been spoiled for time. "No—I can't live on land—!" is the last thing he says before lurching off to board his ship.

The poet considers the broken sailor a survivor from an era in which seafaring stirred men from matter-of-fact complacency to a receptiveness to the Ideal. The sea had not then been subdued by the machine; it challenged all the courage and skill of individuals, and it rewarded them by leaving traces of its majesty upon their consciousness. As the poet "started walking home across the Bridge," he saw in his imagination not steamships but clippers and square-riggers. Aloft over the vast harbor, he envisioned the impact of the sea upon America in the past. Tacking schooners, sailors' chanteys, names and record runs in oceanic rivalries appear in a scene resplendent with the might and beauty of a bygone time.

> Pennants, parabolas—
> clipper dreams indelible and ranging,
> baronial white on lucky blue!
>
> Perennial—*Cutty*—trophied—*Sark!*

"Cape Hatteras"

The section "Cape Hatteras" concludes the survey of cardinal epochs in American history. Its subject is appropriate to modern times—the conquest of space. After the evocation in the preceding sections of the spiritual implications of the land and the sea, "Cape Hatteras" explores the final element to challenge man. The archetypal modern achievement—man's ability to fly—is considered for its significance to the human spirit.

The poem is also a tribute to Walt Whitman. His idealistic outlook animates *The Bridge*; in "Cape Hatteras" it is acknowledged. Whitman appears at this point because he was especially hospitable to modern inventions. He believed in the power of technical advances to convey the ideal. Accordingly, Crane felt his support most keenly in this section and gratefully expressed his indebtedness:

> Our Meistersinger, thou set breath in steel;
> And it was thou who on the boldest heel
> Stood up and flung the span on even wing
> Of that great Bridge, our Myth, whereof I sing!

Thus, the dual intention of "Cape Hatteras" is to suggest the idealism at the core of man's mechanical triumphs and to pay tribute to Walt Whitman, the American poet most responsive to this truth. Crane's technique was to create startling images of the modern mechanical age and to intersperse them with invocations to Whitman as a prophet of new states of consciousness and as the loving companion of those who seek them.

To a remarkable degree, the poem fulfills this intention. Its defects are those of excess, a failure of the poet to know when to stop. The poem strains for an effect and, in doing so, is weakened by overstatement. For example, modern man's preoccupation with machinery and space is insisted upon at such length that the reader wearies. It is first announced that:

> Now the eagle dominates our days, is jurist
> Of the ambiguous cloud. We know the strident rule
> Of wings imperious . . .

Next, man's dependence upon machinery for the realization of his dream of conquering space is expressed: "The nasal whine of power whips a new universe." Then, in trying to suggest the automatic frenzy of "power's script," the poet succumbs to an alliterative orgy and loses power. After being "stropped to the slap of belts on booming spools, spurred / Into the bulging bouillon, harnessed jelly of the stars. / . . . in whirling armatures / As bright as frogs' eyes, giggling in the girth / Of steely gizzards," the reader is not only exhausted but sceptical. He suspects the poet's knowledge and faith in his material.

The tribute to Whitman suffers from the same weakness because it exceeds the grounds on which Whitman may deservedly be praised. Crane's decision to praise Whitman in this section was apt. Of all our poets, Whitman faced the "Years of the Modern" most gladly. In the lines expressing this relationship, the results are persuasive. But, when Crane's panegyric exceeds this point, the poem suffers. He allows himself to celebrate Whitman as the merciful wound-dresser and even more unexpectedly as a nature-god, *"Panis Angelicus"*! These accolades are ill-placed in an exploration of mechanics and air travel. They are sentimental and probably result from Crane's anxiety about the strength of his material. Fearful that his tribute to Whitman as the "joyous seer" would seem weak, he added praises that distract from the real strength of the section.

"Three Songs"

"Three Songs" deals with love as the basis and motive for idealism. In the preceding sections love has been recognized but subordinated to the evocation of particular episodes. It sustained Columbus during his journey and led him to accept God's way of searching "cruelly with love thy parable of man." In "The Harbor Dawn" sexual union symbolizes the realization of the spiritual promise of the land. So, too, love binds the hoboes and the Indian to the continent, and Whitman is revered for having kept his "eyes tranquil with the blaze / Of love's own diametric gaze, of love's amaze!" In "Three Songs" love itself is the subject. The epigraph is from Marlowe's *Hero and Leander*: "The one Sestos, the other Abydos hight"—the towns in which the separated lovers lived on each side of the Hellespont. Leander attempted to fulfill his desire by making his body a bridge of love. A similar attempt and the difficulties endured in its behalf by a modern seeker are presented in the three lyrics of this section: "Southern Cross," "National Winter Garden," and "Virginia."

In "Southern Cross" the poet admits having experienced only carnality in his pursuit of ideal love. "I wanted you," he cries out twice, and clearly indicates that his desire transcended fleshliness. He sought the "nameless Woman of the South, / No wraith, but utterly," and he envisioned his satisfaction as "wide from the slowly smouldering fire / Of lower heavens." He has yearned for "Mary"—pure love—but has found Eve instead. The fallen woman, "simian Venus, homeless Eve," is the terrible symbol of his failure.

This confession is made while the poet is journeying at night in southern waters. He has aspired to reach the Southern Cross, symbol of sublime fulfillment, but thus far his only fruition has been sensual. His supplication of the stars "falls vainly on the wave" and joins the wake of the vessel, the "furrow of all our travel—trailed derision!" He recognizes the sterility of those who fail to transcend the senses: "Unwedded, stumbling gardenless to grieve / Windswept guitars on lonely decks forever; / Finally to answer all within one grave!" He sees himself in this plight and is compelled to listen to its "whispering hell."

The contrast between his desire and his experience provides the structure of the poem. It is established in the lines already quoted and is then repeated more tersely and with greater impact. The same clause, "I wanted you," introduces the second cycle. The constellation is yearned for as the reward for enduring love's torment: "The embers of the Cross / Climbed by aslant and huddling aromatically." Once more he finds only Eve with her "rehearsed hair," the "wraith of my unloved seed!" The onset of dawn ends his vision but provides no resolution to the conflict:

> The Cross, a phantom, buckled—dropped below the dawn.
> Light drowned the lithic trillions of your spawn.

"National Winter Garden" is like "Southern Cross"—in reverse. In "Southern Cross" the reader is introduced to a pure ideal and then confronted by sordid reality; in "National Winter Garden" the limelights of a burlesque show are thrown upon the "flagrant, sweating cinch" of sensuality, but at the end the power of even lasciviousness to advance the quest for spirituality is recognized.

In burlesque, sensuality is shamelessly flaunted; there are "no extra mufflings here." The ritualistic ceremony described in "The Dance" is parodied and reduced to fleshliness. Idealism is trampled in a "tom-tom scrimmage" of vulgarity and prurience. "Her silly snake rings begin to mount, surmount / Each other— turquoise fakes on tinselled hands." Her ecstasy is fraudulent; she mimics passion and knows none of its agonies: "Least tearful and least glad (who knows her smile?) / A caught slide shows her sandstone grey between."

The poet searches for the meaning of her performance. He feels the incitement of fleshliness, but at the same time he recognizes· that he seeks more than fleshly satisfaction. He desires the spiritualization of his concupiscence. Although he picks a "blonde out neatly through the smoke," he reminds himself that "always you wait for someone else though, always." Besides, the sensuality of the dance destroys itself by excess. The possibility of realizing a spiritual ideal under such physical pressure seems foregone. He is led to reject the flesh and to pursue a disembodied ideal: "We flee her spasm through a fleshless door."

He then recognizes that flight from sensuality is as barren as the obsession with it in the burlesque. Love cannot be exclusively spiritual or physical. It must attain its fulfillment through the senses, not at their expense. This insight enables him to see the dancer differently. She is now addressed as Magdalene—the harlot whose power of love carried her to the feet of Christ. Although the dancer offers no fulfillment in "the empty trapeze" of her flesh, she does help us by arousing—even if only to frustrate—not only our lust but our faith in love. She mimics an ecstasy that is spiritual as well as physical. Although her performance is false and causes all who see it "to die alone," she suggests a fulfillment that is real. In doing this, she rekindles a desire that her dance has failed to satisfy. By this route she is able to "lug us back lifeward—bone by infant bone."

After the conflict between the flesh and the spirit that burdens the first two songs, "Virginia" lilts beguilingly of romance. It celebrates a youthful and tender image of love. Happily its presentation is so winsome that sentimentality is avoided.

The title suggests the spirit of this piece: love is virginal, glimmering with the promise of ideal realization. The degradations of love are unknown. The personification of love is Mary; the taint of Eve and Magdalene, fallen women, is absent. Mary dwells in purity high in a tower like Rapunzel or, as the title suggests, like the Virgin Mary. The poet is a suppliant modestly invoking the realization of his ideal. He pleads for her favor but can impose no stronger claim: "I'm still waiting you," "O Mary, leaning from the high wheat tower, / Let down your golden hair!" "Shine, / Cathedral Mary, / shine!—"

"Virginia" charmingly locates its invocation to ideal love within modern circumstances. It confirms the promise of the entire poem that currents of idealism continue despite the conditions of modern life. Cathedral Mary is a working girl in the Woolworth Building, and the poet is her boy friend waiting for her to quit work at noon on Saturday. He courts her in the jaunty rhythm of a popular love song:

> O blue-eyed Mary with the claret scarf,
> Saturday Mary, mine!

His love transforms the commonplace features of lower Manhattan: "green figs gleam / By oyster shells" in Prince Street; "crap shooting gangs in Bleecker reign," along with "peonies with pony manes— / Forget-me-nots at windowpanes." In the "shine" of love's splendid promise, all the commotion of city streets is transfigured.

"Quaker Hill"

The theme of love is continued in "Quaker Hill," but it is presented in a new way. Instead of the conflict between love and sensuality, the difficulty of achieving an idealistic expression of love in modern times is considered. As in "Three Songs," women portray the face of love. The time is modern, and the archetypal women—Eve, Magdalene, and Mary—are replaced by the Americans Emily Dickinson and Isadora Duncan. They represent the refinement of love; they were aware of the spirituality at the heart of matter. Their fate in society is the subject of the poem.

The theme is anticipated by the epigraphs. One is a forthright indictment of "the world" by Isadora Duncan: "I see only the ideal. But no ideals have ever been fully successful on this earth." The other is an excerpt from an elegy to summer by Emily Dickinson: "The gentian weaves her fringes, / The maple's loom is red." Loneliness, disregard, and pain were inflicted upon these sensitive women by a crude society.

The cause of their pain is presented by the poet in a bitter depiction of modern vulgarity. He describes a country scene in New England, an area associated for him with the days when it was considered the Promised Land, the New Jerusalem, but one now put to such vulgar use that the cows seem to be the only wholesome creatures there. An old Quaker Meeting

House is now the New Avalon Hotel, providing "a welcome to highsteppers that no mouse / Who saw the Friends there ever heard before." The land has been barbered into a golf course where players "in plaid plusfours / Alight with sticks abristle and cigars." The people are envious of each other and indifferent to nature. They cheapen the countryside with their drinking and vulgar interest in antiques. In their midst the poet, who feels isolated from the roots that once nourished America, cries plaintively, "Where are my kinsmen and the patriarch race?" He suffers "the curse of sundered parentage"; instead of being sustained by close bonds with the past, he is cut off from it.

His anguish enables him to understand the "pain that Emily, that Isadora knew!" Their noble spirits were forced to bow to frailty and death.

> So, must we from the hawk's far stemming view,
> Must we descend as worm's eye to construe
> Our love of all we touch . . .

Society and nature rebuff idealism in much the same way. Everyone must "take this sheaf of dust" upon his tongue and accept the fleeting passage of love's fulfillment in time. Nature inevitably suffers its autumnal decay. This knowledge "breaks us" by discouraging our strongest desire, but it should also help us to accept our descent into time with—

> That patience that is armour and that shields
> Love from despair—when love foresees the end—

"The Tunnel"

In "The Tunnel" modern society is visualized as the lower world, hell—appropriately symbolized by the subway. Visiting the lower world is a daily ordeal for the city dweller.

The screaming descent of the subway into the earth mocks man's desire to rise above it. How can the quest for spirituality be realized by pilgrims who are thrust underground continually amid a society that seems to want no better fate? The fierce impingement of matter immolates the spirit and requires its daily resurrection. Yet this assault is seen as a fit challenge to idealism, for it prevents anyone from indulging a naïve and vulnerable faith in the human spirit. An ideal must be pursued despite the strongest obstacles to it. If there is a heaven, evidence must be found for it even in hell.

The poet has been in Times Square facing its night-time bombardment of "performances, assortments, résumés—" and is on his way home. "The subway yawns the quickest promise home"; he enters the underground. Movement, sound, sight are mingled chaotically; fragments of conversation strike him. Nothing makes sense, and the total effect is crass. Love, the dominant topic, is reduced to a tawdry function.

> The phonographs of hades in the brain
> Are tunnels that re-wind themselves, and love
> A burnt match skating in a urinal—

In this shambles, the poet feels torn apart, like Orpheus: "Whose head is swinging from the swollen strap? / Whose body smokes along the bitten rails?" He associates his agony with Poe's; they are both poets seeking the ideal and suffering in its behalf. He sees "Death, aloft,—gigantically down / Probing through you—toward me, O evermore!"

The train then drops to its lowest point under the river. It is "demented, for a hitching second, humps; then / Lets go." This moment of the train's surrender to its farthest descent is critical for the poet. He responds by abandoning himself to despair and death. He faces his destroyer bitterly—not God but "Daemon"—and derides man's spiritual hunger as a hideous jest.

> O cruelly to inoculate the brinking dawn
> With antennae toward worlds that glow and sink;—
> To spoon us out more liquid than the dim
> Locution of the eldest star, and pack
> The conscience navelled in the plunging wind,
> Umbilical to call—and straightway die!

The train then reverses its direction and heads for the surface. "Like Lazarus" it has been buried and now begins "to feel the slope / The sod and billow breaking,—lifting ground." This alteration revives the poet's hope. He is encouraged to believe that in his consciousness there exists "some Word that will not die!" The ascent of the train may portend his own resurrection after his ordeal. He is still uncertain but hopeful, and what had earlier been a rebuke to the "Daemon" for tormenting men with the futile desire for the ideal becomes a dedication of himself to its realization:

> Kiss of our agony Thou gatherest,
> O Hand of Fire
> gatherest—

"Atlantis"

"Atlantis" presents the vital image of the entire poem. Though properly placed at the end of *The Bridge,* it was the first section to be completed. It expresses the poet's ecstasy upon discovering the Brooklyn Bridge to be a symbol of his spiritual faith. Through the union of Crane's creative intuition and the evocative power of the bridge, this artifact became a promise and a foretaste of spiritual fulfillment. It led to Atlantis—the perfect land of his desire, the goal of his quest for a sign that modern times could "lend a myth to God." Having experienced this encouragement, he was transformed from an estranged man to a missionary. He found other evidences to support his faith throughout American history, but his witness rested fundamentally upon the metamorphosis of the Brooklyn Bridge into a spiritual reality.

The epigraph from Plato suggests the dominant features of the transfigured bridge: "Music is then the knowledge of that which relates to love in harmony and system." The bridge affirms and advances the poet's faith because it is an epiphany of love and music. Throughout the section, musical images are used; the bridge is both an instrument and the harmony played upon it. The cables reverberate like a harp to the spiritual rhythms of nature and society: "Sibylline voices flicker, waveringly stream / As though a god were issue of the strings." These are not ordinary sounds but "new octaves" that respond to the deepest impulses of creation. The structure consists of "arching strands of song!" It is a "Choir," the "One Song," the "Psalm of Cathay" whose "orphic strings" are needed by the poet to inspire his faltering efforts at harmony.

The theme sounded upon the "humming spars" and "deathless

strings" is love. All the lessons of history and the meaning of nature's flow through time are expressed in the cry of the bridge: "Make thy love sure—to weave whose song we ply!" This is the goal of man's groping and the sacred gospel of the poem: to become a "Bridge to Thee, O Love." This love is absolute, secure from the mutability of time.

> And like an organ, Thou, with sound of doom—
> Sight, sound and flesh Thou leadest from time's realm
> As love strikes clear direction for the helm.

Because love guides its disciples out of time to the pure fulfillment of God, and is itself the face of God, the images of these spiritual absolutes merge interchangeably. "Bridge," "Love," "multitudinous Verb," "steeled Cognizance," "Myth," "Atlantis," and simply "Thou" struggle to designate the mysterious union of absolutes.

The poet humbly submits to this vision. Recognizing that its appeal and truth are 'iridescently upborne / Through the bright drench and fabric of our veins," he knows also the difficulty of realizing it: "Eyes stammer through the pangs of dust and steel." The claims of matter are enduring, and faith is always subject to doubt. He is thankful for the encouragement he has received; its "canticle fresh chemistry assigns / To rapt inception and beatitude." Now his success will depend upon his ability to continue to hear "Deity's young name" among the "white escarpments" of the bridge. He accepts the pain that this pursuit will entail: crossing the bridge will take him "from gulfs unfolding, terrible of drums" and lead him "through smoking pyres of love and death."

In the last metamorphosis of the bridge, it becomes the "whitest Flower," the anemone; and its sun-washed petals rise radiantly from the ocean of time like Atlantis. Before the splendor of this apparition, the poet asks "pardon for this history." He is overwhelmed by the inadequacy of his words to echo his ecstasy and begs that the currents of his inspiration will "hold thy floating singer late!"

The poem ends by praising the vision to which the poet has dedicated himself:

So to thine Everpresence, beyond time,
Like spears ensanguined of one tolling star
That bleeds infinity—the orphic strings,
Sidereal phalanxes, leap and converge:
—One Song, one Bridge of Fire! . . .

VI *Crane's Achievement*

Crane's organization of American history in *The Bridge* is
based upon an extended analogy. He refers to many events, but
they are all used to illustrate the same insight. His interest
was not in their relationship but in their availability as *exempla*
of his theme. Each episode is put to the task of revealing
its bearing upon idealism; other significances are either dis-
regarded or subordinated. This is the method of the sermon,
not of history or myth. The subject—idealism—is universal; its
presentation is furnished with American examples so that its
appeal to American readers will be increased. Although a particular theme might be shown by its recurrence and intensity to
typify American experience and, consequently, to express the
"meaning" of America, this demonstration is not made in *The
Bridge.*

The Bridge conveys a desire for spiritual fulfillment but
not its realization. Any expectation that it presents a "mystical"
experience is bound to be disappointed. The closest the poem
approaches any such achievement is in "Atlantis"; there the
poet is illumined by ecstasy, but not the ecstasy of being in
union with the divine. He is enraptured by the power of the
Brooklyn Bridge to symbolize a junction of time and the timeless.
The beauty of the bridge is transformed into the beauty of a path
to eternity. In its glow he experiences an anticipation of the
fulfillment waiting at the farther end, and he prays that he
will be permitted to journey toward it. His creative intuition
is limited to the possibility of reaching the Absolute. Thus
The Bridge is not a poem of fulfillment—no *Divine Comedy*—but
of need and desire. Its appeal lies in its manifestation of how
deep man's dissatisfaction with temporal conditions really is
and how indomitable is his groping for a higher state.

Recognizing that the focus of *The Bridge* is upon desire rather than fulfillment helps to determine Crane's success in arousing our faith in the realization of his quest. This question is crucial, for, as several of his statements have shown, he regarded *The Bridge* chiefly as an affirmative refutation of the negativism of his time. Unfortunately, *The Bridge* does not fulfill Crane's intention. His desire for absolute beauty and love is established, but the confidence of the reader in his ever achieving it is not. This failure is not due to the reader's prejudice, for even when read with sympathy for the poet's quest, the poem leaves a pessimistic impression. The reader respects the poet's yearning but cannot anticipate his success.

The principal explanation of the ironic fact that a poem aiming consciously at fostering hopefulness results in depression is that it reveals a loss of confidence in its premise. So many admissions of personal and cultural barriers to idealism are made that the reader is persuaded that they are insurmountable. The weight of sensuality and materialism seems too heavy for the poet to give wing to his noble aspiration. The vision of "Atlantis" glimmers as an irresistible goal, but the condition of the poet seems too anchored in "The Tunnel," "Quaker Hill," and "National Winter Garden" for it to be achieved. The conviction grows that Crane began the poem on the impulse of the extraordinary illumination of "Atlantis" but that, in trying to realize its promise, he met discouragement that he was too honest to dissemble and too weak to overcome. The vision never ceased goading him to struggle for its fulfillment, but his strength was unequal to the task. *The Bridge* testifies to the poet's incessant desire for the Absolute—and the tenacity of his desire may be the strongest encouragement to hopefulness offered by the poem—but also to his tacit foreknowledge of failure.

CHAPTER 5

"Voyages"

AFTER THE SUCCESS of "Faustus and Helen" in 1923, Crane
left Cleveland and settled in New York City. He felt that
his apprenticeship was over and that he was ready for major
accomplishments. Plans for *The Bridge* were being drawn—his
friends received almost daily reports of his progress—and visions
of its splendor kept him exhilarated with anticipation. He pre-
dicted to Munson: "If I do succeed, such a waving of banners,
such ascent of towers, such dancing, etc., will never before have
been put down on paper!"[1]

After a few exciting weeks of leisure, his money was almost
gone and he faced the problem of employment—a vexation that
plagued him for the rest of his life. Lacking an independent
income he was forced to work, and the only work he was
experienced at—advertising—sapped his creative energy. When
unemployed, he was crippled for poetry by financial worries;
when employed, he was too exhausted to write poetry. In
addition, he grew increasingly anxious about the welfare of
his mother and grandmother, the affection of his father, and
the loyalty and constancy of his friends.

He soon suffered the impoverishment of the impulse that
had brought him to New York. Joyful anticipations of success
ceased, and so did work itself. After a productive period
in July, 1923, when he drafted about forty lines of "Atlantis,"
the work lay fallow for about three years. It was not until the
summer of 1926, while on the Isle of Pines, Cuba, that his
creative fervor returned.

Ironically, the difficulties that postponed the completion of *The Bridge* occasioned the finest lyrics of his first volume, *White Buildings* (1926). Poems like "Possessions," "Recitative," "Lachrymae Christi," "At Melville's Tomb," and most particularly "Voyages" are eloquent outcries of his quest for love and spiritual wholeness. But Crane regarded these poems as merely interim pieces written while the construction of his masterwork was halted; he said of them: "I am working still on *The Bridge,* but it is far from complete yet. In the meantime I am working on some smaller poems that crop out from time to time very naturally."[2] Nonetheless, he paid them the respect that shows in the power of the work itself.

Actually, the short lyric was the most appropriate for Crane's poetic sensibility. His intense emotional reaction to experience, his impatience with the rules of discursive reasoning, his indifference to "facts," his desire to articulate new states of consciousness, his belief that poetry should present an experience rather than make a report about it, and his wish to concentrate as many facets into his poems as are found in experience—all these traits point toward a compact, personal form of self-revelation. Indeed, as we have seen, he came eventually to recognize this truth about himself following the publication of *The Bridge.*

As Crane's most profound insights were experienced in searching for love and his deepest fascination was for the sea, his most luminous work was achieved in "Voyages," a sequence of six lyrics in which the mysteries of these two subjects are fused. The occasion was a homosexual relationship carried on in an apartment overlooking New York harbor and intensified by the intervals when his friend was at sea. It lasted only from the spring to the fall of 1924, but it kept Crane in an ecstasy of tenderness and doubt. He wrote to Waldo Frank of his exaltation: "I have seen the Word made Flesh. I mean nothing less, and I know now that there is such a thing as indestructibility. In the deepest sense, where flesh became transformed through intensity of response to counter-response, where sex was beaten out, where a purity of joy was reached that included tears." He went on to associate, even to identify, this personal experience with the sea: "I think the sea has thrown itself upon me and been answered, at least in part, and I believe I am a little changed—not essentially, but changed and transubstantiated as anyone is who has asked a question and been answered."[3]

I   *"Poster"*

In the fall of 1924, Crane first mentioned the literary result of this relationship in a letter to his mother: "I'm engaged in writing a series of six sea poems called 'Voyages' (they are also love poems)."[4] He decided to use a poem written prior to "Faustus and Helen" as the introductory piece of the series. It was "Poster," which, as has already been explained, expressed a warning in Melvillean imagery of land and sea that, although the surface of life may seem benign, dangers threaten those who attempt to explore its depths.

II   *"And yet this great wink of eternity"*

The second "Voyage" exempts lovers from the cruelty of the sea. The danger of the depths of the sea persists, "and yet" for lovers the sea is not a grave but "this great wink of eternity." The sea symbolizes a timeless plane of love. It is described in images of passion and fecundity, "rimless floods, unfettered leewardings, / Samite sheeted and processioned where / Her undinal vast belly moonward bends." On the strength of its amorous nature, the poet feels confident of the sea's benevolence toward his personal relationship. He imagines its "laughing the wrapt inflections of our love."

In the second stanza, the contrast between the imperious despotism of the sea and its indulgence of lovers is heightened. The sea is described as a magistrate from whose verdicts no appeal may be made. "Take this Sea, whose diapason knells / On scrolls of silver snowy sentences, / The sceptred terror of whose sessions rends / As her demeanors motion well or ill."[5] Only "the pieties of lovers' hands" receive its constant sympathy.

In the next two stanzas the nature of the sea is more closely explored in order to understand its partiality toward lovers. The poet discovers that the sea contains an intimation of love's ideal fulfillment. In the movement of its tides around ·

the "poinsettia meadows" of tropical islands and in the sound of the "bells off San Salvador" as they "salute the crocus lustres of the stars," he finds the completion of the "dark confessions" of its foam-lashed depths. The oneness of the sea as "her turning shoulders wind the hours," the thrust of her waves toward the stars, and the glowing beauty of her islands symbolize love's quest for fulfillment in time and hint that its realization can occur only in eternity. The sea suggests that submission to human love is the only way to realize both the limits of love and its power to prefigure spiritual satisfactions. The poet learns that he must hasten to accept the paradox that "sleep, death, desire, / Close round one instant in one floating flower." Love's power is to bring the temporal into contact with the eternal through the impulse of desire.

Overwhelmed by this intuition, the poet prays that he may live long and passionately enough to achieve the awareness of eternity that the sea portends. He accepts the dangers of love in order to learn its secret.

> Bind us in time, O Seasons clear, and awe.
> O minstrel galleons of Carib fire,
> Bequeath us to no earthly shore until
> Is answered in the vortex of our grave
> The seal's wide spindrift gaze toward paradise.

III *"Infinite consanguinity it bears"*

"Voyages III" continues the exploration of the bond between the sea and love. The poet resumes "this tendered theme": starting from the perception of the "infinite consanguinity it bears," he recognizes that the sea is the element of love. It transports his beloved: "a breast that every wave enthrones." It is also the element of death; though tender, "the sea lifts, also, reliquary hands." He sees that, to find love, he must surrender himself to the sea. Through its depths he will search for his beloved, even if his requital means self-immolation.

> . . . ribboned water lanes I wind
> Are laved and scattered with no stroke
> Wide from your side. . . .

At this point in the voyage of love, attraction has been felt and may advance toward fulfillment only if the lover abandons himself to love's uncharted course. He must let himself into the sea and yield to its currents. Transformation demands submission to a dangerous element. "Full fathom five thy father lies / . . . And those are pearls that were his eyes," Shakespeare wrote in *The Tempest,* a play Crane thought the "crown of all the Western world."[6]

Aware of his peril, the poet drops into the sea. He passes through its "black swollen gates," and enters a new world; old sureties slip asunder, and he finds that the route to exaltation is through depth. His only guide is his desire for his beloved who waits somewhere for him.

> And so, admitted through black swollen gates
> That must arrest all distance otherwise,—
> Past whirling pillars and lithe pediments,
> Light wrestling there incessantly with light,
> Star kissing star through wave on wave unto
> Your body rocking!

He accepts the danger of this pursuit the more readily because of his insight into the special nature of death suffered for love. It is not the destructive, disintegrating process of nature but a process of transformation. Love inflicts a martyrdom that sanctifies. In its cause "death, if shed, / Presumes no carnage." In the purifying, rhythmic caress of the sea, death would work only "this single change" upon a lover:

> Upon the steep floor flung from dawn to dawn
> The silken skilled transmemberment of song

This presentiment inspires the lover. He fears only that he is not worthy of such a privilege. He concludes by humbly supplicating love to approve his quest: "Permit me voyage, love, into your hands. . . ."

Crane's artistry and insight reach their zenith in this poem. Its images are so apt for both love and the sea that the poem may be read with each separately in mind and no detail seems inappropriate. So, too, does the rhythm accord perfectly with its two burdens. Thematically, it is his most concentrated expression of idealism. With a dynamism fully as suggestive as Eliot's handling of the same theme in *The Waste Land,* Crane evokes the implications of death by water. Eliot used drowning as a symbol of rebirth in grace and immortality; Crane used it to symbolize the ideal fulfillment of love.

IV *"Whose counted smile of hours and days, suppose"*

Having committed himself to love's journey, the poet anticipates its requital in "Voyages IV." He imagines the sea, which at the moment separates him from his beloved, to be the bond of love. Its flow overcomes distance and unites lovers as intimately as when they are actually together.

He associates the "spectrum of the sea" with the "counted smile" of his beloved that he must still await through "hours and days." As the sun reflects the passage of time, so does he tell the hours until his beloved shall return. As he penetrates the analogue of the sea, more of its implications are unfolded. He recognizes that it is a "pledge" of love's fulfillment, both physically at some later time and immediately through its power to transmit spiritual impulses. Even though it seems to be "vastly now parting gulf on gulf of wings," it is not divisive. It conveys the pulsations of love instantaneously and also employs the wings of sea birds to form a bridge "from palms to the severe / Chilled albatross's white immutability." Beneath this arc passes

> No stream of greater love advancing now
> Than, singing, this mortality alone
> Through clay aflow immortally to you.

Love and poetry and the sea have united to overcome the limitations of matter.

On the surge of this vision, the poet experiences an intimation of fulfillment. He receives a foretaste of love's requital, undeniable despite the paradox of union in solitude. It includes "all fragrance irrefragibly, and claim / Madly meeting logically in this hour." Simultaneously it prefigures the union "that is ours to wreathe again, / Portending eyes and lips and making told / The chancel port and portion of our June." This imaginary experience seems so real that it includes the suffering, the "bright staves of flowers and quills," that accompany satisfaction in love. These are the signs of love, but their recognition awaits the insight of one who "must first be lost in fatal tides to tell."

In the necessary relationship between suffering and love, the power of love to realize the "incarnate word" is associated with the sea's office of "mingling / Mutual blood." The sea is the timeless element in which human efforts toward fulfillment transpire "as foreknown." It is also apocalyptic; it reveals the spirituality of human experience. In this instance, it makes the absent lover more receptive to "gathering / All bright insinuations that my years have caught," and it prepares the poet "for islands where must lead inviolably / Blue latitudes and levels of your eyes." These visions thrill the poet and strengthen his hope. They enable him to feel confident of his ultimate satisfaction. "In this expectant," he avows, summing up the exaltation and self-surrender anticipated in the poem:

> . . . still exclaim receive
> The secret oar and petals of all love.

V   *"Meticulous, past midnight in clear rime"*

In "Voyages V" the promised mysteries of love's fulfillment—"the secret oar and petals of all love"—are replaced by unmistakable signs of the death of love. The harmony upon which the attainment of ecstasy depended has been broken. No longer are two people united in love. Although they are still in each other's company, the spiritual distance between them has widened beyond bridging. The poet resumes his loneliness with resignation and grief.

He indicates how clearly he recognizes his loss. The night that had been crowded with annunciations has now but one message—loneliness. "Meticulous, past midnight in clear rime, / Infrangible and lonely, smooth as though cast / Together in one merciless white blade— / The bay estuaries fleck the hard sky limits." The loss of love is established also in the imagery of a bridge. Together the lovers had been exalted; now "the cables of our sleep so swiftly filed, / Already hang, shred ends from remembered stars." It is too late even for commemoration in language, for "what words / Can strangle this deaf moonlight?"

The change that has altered the communion of the lovers is emphasized by references to the moon. Whereas formerly it represented fecundity—the sea's "undinal vast belly moonward bends,"—it is now "deaf," a "tidal wedge" driving the lovers apart; they suffer its "slow tyranny," "moonlight loved / And changed." The poet's grief is explained by the adjective "tidal": "Now no cry, no sword / Can fasten or deflect this tidal wedge." The moon not only marks the passage of time but it influences the tides that summon the beloved. The end of the idyl has come.

It is not merely that the beloved must go to sea once again. Parting has been endured before and could be borne again if faith in their spiritual union remained firm. This faith has been lost, and now suspicion drives the lovers apart more effectively than the sea. The poet surmises that his beloved is relieved to be on his way, that already he is anticipating experiences that they will never share. He fears betrayal and cannot accept the beloved's insisting, "There's / Nothing like this in the world." He suspects that it is only a polite way of saying goodbye: "Knowing I cannot touch your hand and look / Too, into that godless cleft of sky / Where nothing turns but dead sands flashing." He has given his love and now must watch it being carried away by someone who is careless of it. Bitterly he protests:

> In all the argosy of your bright hair I dreamed
> Nothing so flagless as this piracy.

He accepts defeat. He recognizes that love demands a mutual self-surrender and cannot endure with less. Efforts to prolong what is already dead or to protest what cannot be altered are futile. Lovers cannot be tied; they must bind themselves. He gives up his claim and his hope; he yields his beloved to a destiny he cannot share. They have been parted in spirit; he offers his valediction to the separation of their bodies:

> But now
> Draw in your head, alone and too tall here.
> Your eyes already in the slant of drifting foam;

Your breath sealed by the ghosts I do not know:
Draw in your head and sleep the long way home.

VI *"Where icy and bright dungeons lift"*

It is not surprising that Crane extended "Voyages" beyond
this melancholy pass. Although he was candid in admitting the
failure of his personal relationships, he never lost faith in
ideal love. Love was the goal of his aspiration. Efforts to achieve
it might collapse, but the attractiveness and value of the goal
stood firm. In "Voyages VI" he pays tribute to this ideal. Begun
years earlier as "Belle Isle," it consists of two parts: a humble
declaration of his desire for love and an ecstatic vision of its
pure and absolute realization.

The medium is still the sea. Exaltation comes from surrender
to it, and spiritual ascent from descent into its depths. The
sea reaches upward and carries with it those who yield themselves to its flow: "Icy and bright dungeons lift / Of swimmers
their lost morning eyes." There is a bond between the sea and the
sky. Just as water ascends to the heavens in spray and mist,
so may men be exalted. The poet is encouraged by the perception that "waters trough the sun's / Red kelson", and he sees
"rivers mingling toward the sky / And harbor of the phoenix'
breast." In these symbols he finds his salvation and he humbly
begs to be borne by the sea:

> My eyes pressed black against the prow,
> —Thy derelict and blinded guest
>
> Waiting, afire, what name, unspoke,
> I cannot claim: let thy waves rear
> More savage than the death of kings,
> Some splintered garland for the seer.

He seeks a goal that he cannot name but which his desire impels
him to pursue. He knows only that it surpasses all transitory
things, that it is the "harbor of the phoenix' breast."

His supplication is rewarded by a vision of his goal. Far
"beyond siroccos harvesting," he enjoys an image of the spiritual
realm of beauty and love. It is a tropical island, "Belle Isle,"

glowing with ideal loveliness. It is "creation's blithe and petalled word / To the lounged goddess when she rose" and the true "white echo of the oar." "The secret oar and petals of all love" had been sought in "Voyages IV" in a human relationship. That relationship had failed, but the ideal remains and is realized in Belle Isle. The island is eternity's "still fervid covenant" with men, an "unfolded floating dais before / Which rainbows twine continual hair." It is a pledge of enduring fulfillment; its constancy impels the poet to offer his utmost homage. In words charged with religious and personal significance, he ends his celebration:

> The imaged Word, it is, that holds
> Hushed willows anchored in its glow.
> It is the unbetrayable reply
> Whose accent no farewell can know.

In this ecstasy, he envisions his harbor, the goal of his voyages. It is the pure possession that he had long sought but had failed to experience. It dwelled always at the heart of his desire. His failure to realize it could not extinguish its glow; it beckoned to him even in the throes of his worst defeats.

VII *"Voyages" as Self-exploration*

The "Voyages" sequence was placed at the end of *White Buildings* and brought the volume to a splendid conclusion. The concentration and intimate self-exploration of these six poems effect a powerful lyricism. Their reach does not extend beyond their strength. Even though they are charged with meanings that are difficult to perceive simultaneously and that at times cohere in defiance of syntax, they are not forced. They do not seem false; they express the richness of a deeply felt experience.

These poems succeed better than some earlier and later ones because they are at once personal, modest, and candid. Crane's own experience was his best subject. His power of vision was sharpest when used introspectively. He fathomed the workings of his own psyche with clarity and penetration; his presentation of other people's experiences generally seems superficial. These poems are mirrors of himself; as in "Recitative," he "crust[s] a plate of vibrant mercury / Borne cleft to you, and brother in the half." He offers self-portraits, and because they are true they reach a depth of common human significance. Crane demonstrates the paradox of the romantic artist: he reveals most about other men when he is most self-absorbed.

Despite the frequent claim that Crane was a mystic, these poems simply show his yearning for the Absolute. He did not claim fulfillment; he desired it and anticipated it in radiant images. These poems are not reports of transfiguration on the holy mount but testimony of Crane's dissatisfaction with life on the plain and of his faith in the possibility of climbing higher. At times the persistence of his faith seems remarkable, but he never substitutes fruition for desire. He is candid in admitting failure and weakness. Crane drops a plummet into his personal experience and does not hesitate to report its soundings.

CHAPTER 6

Crane and His Critics

IT IS APPROPRIATE that Hart Crane's most influential critics—
Yvor Winters, Allen Tate, and R. P. Blackmur—have emphasized his intuitive poetic and his thematic quest for visions of
the Absolute, but it is regrettable that they have found these
elements fatal to his poetry. They have seen his creative method
and intentions as illustrative of a romanticism they repudiate,
and they have concluded that even his extraordinary talent
could not overcome the false premises to which he had committed it. By reasoning in this way, they have been led to
undervalue Crane's work and to base their judgments upon an
unduly narrow critical position. Fairness to Crane and to the
type of poetry that he presents requires a serious modification
of their analysis.

I *Romanticism Indicted by Winters*

The negative view of romanticism taken by Crane's critics
is presented in its most extreme form in the work of Yvor
Winters. His volumes *Primitivism and Decadence* (1937), *Maule's
Curse* (1938), and *The Anatomy of Nonsense* (1943), together
with his essay, "The Significance of *The Bridge* by Hart Crane,"
have been published collectively under the title, *In Defense
of Reason* (1947)—altogether a sweeping indictment of romanticism and its modern offspring. Winters writes, of course,
only for himself, and his views are far more rigid and severe
than Tate's and Blackmur's, even though they share his sus-
picions generally. In the "Foreword" to *In Defense of Reason*,
he states his understanding of the romantic attitude:

The Romantic theory assumes that literature is mainly or even
purely an emotional experience, that man is naturally good, that
man's impulses are trustworthy, that the rational faculty is unreli-

able to the point of being dangerous or possibly evil. The Romantic theory of human nature teaches that if man will rely upon his impulses, he will achieve the good life. When this notion is combined, as it frequently is, with a pantheistic philosophy or religion, it commonly teaches that through surrender to impulse man will not only achieve the good life but will achieve also a kind of mystical union with the Divinity. . . . Literature thus becomes a form of what is known popularly as self-expression.[1]

Winters then proceeds to denounce these romantic assumptions. In *Primitivism and Decadence* he characterizes the attempt to achieve mystical union through surrender to impulse—Crane's endeavor is seen as an attempt of this kind—as a confusion of "subconscious stimuli and reactions with occult inspiration . . . [and] the divine [with] the visceral."[2] Winters doubts man's natural goodness and distrusts man's instincts. He regards reason as man's chief guide and safeguard—not as a menace—and shares the belief expressed in Blackmur's essay on Crane, "New Thresholds, New Anatomies," that "no time could have greater need than our own for rational art."[3] Winters does not believe that the poet has any nonrational route to the Absolute, and he deplores the disregard for logic and literary tradition shown by some poets because of their alleged ecstasies and intuitions. In brief, for Winters romanticism stands for the encouragement of self-indulgence, self-conceit, and literary confusion.

Since Winters is concerned with the romantic tradition in America, he deals mostly with Emerson, Poe, and Whitman. He charges that these men succumbed most fully to the temptations of romanticism and surrendered their talent to its service. He opposes Emerson most severely for bringing an aura of religious and moral propriety to an anarchic viewpoint and for suggesting that "poets are thus liberating gods."[4] He believes that Emerson's theory of inspiration culminates in automatic writing and that, consequently, "Emerson's perfect man is a madman."[5] He considers Whitman a poet of great talent who had the misfortune to accept Emerson's leadership, and he condemns Poe for separating reason from the aesthetic pursuit of beauty and for giving a pseudo-mystical mantle to art. He finds Poe's "The Philosophy of Composition" a "singularly shocking document. . . . it is . . . an effort to establish the rules for a species of incantation, of witchcraft; rules, whereby . . . it may be possible to invoke, more or less accidentally, something that appears more or less to be a divine emanation."[6]

Winters explicitly relates his indictment of romanticism and its principal nineteenth-century American representatives to his criticism of Crane's work. Crane's belief in the intuitive power of the poet to sound a depth of objectivity beyond the reach of reason and his respect for the same earlier American writers whom Winters opposes are used to define his literary position and explain his failure. Winters writes of him as "a poet of great genius, who ruined his life and his talent by living and writing as the two greatest religious teachers of our nation [Emerson and Whitman] recommended."[7] He completes his explanation by finding "the catastrophe of Hart Crane" to be the culmination of "Poe's . . . aesthetic of obscurantism."[8]

II *Tate and Blackmur's Objections*

Similarly, in his essay "Hart Crane," Allen Tate asserts that Crane's "esthetic problem . . . was the historic problem of romanticism."[9] By "esthetic problem" Tate means Crane's quest for transcendent experiences and the steps he took to realize it. He finds Crane's lack of a structure of ideas regrettable, and he deplores the exaltation of this deficiency to the status of a method or a theory. He observes that Crane "falls back upon the intensity of consciousness, rather than clarity, for his center of vision. And that is romanticism."[10] In Crane's efforts to achieve an intuitive grasp of reality through a heightened awareness of his personal experience, Tate sees a solipsistic willfulness irrationally attempting to shape reality to its own design.

His world had no center, and [his] thrust into sensation is responsible for the fragmentary quality of his most ambitious work. . . . Crane could only assert a quality of will against the world, and at each successive failure of the will he turned upon himself. In the failure of understanding . . . the Romantic modern poet of the age of science attempts to impose his will upon experience and to possess the world.[11]

Blackmur, too, distrusts Crane's subordination of reason to intuition. Although he admires Crane's sympathy for the life of words and his ability to quicken them with new meaning, he insists that the absence of rational control precludes a poet's fruitful access to reality. Moreover, he points out that, without a rational structure to work from, the poet is prevented from detecting his own failures. In his essay on D. H. Lawrence, Blackmur warns: "When you depend entirely upon the demon of inspiration, the inner voice, the inner light, you deprive yourself of any external criterion to show whether the demon is working or not."[12] Consequently, in "New Thresholds, New Anatomies" he writes of a "profound duplicity—a deception in the very will of things—in Crane's fundamental attitudes toward his work . . . whereby an accustomed disorder seems the order most to be cherished."[13] Like Winters and Tate, Blackmur feels unable to accord Crane any higher place than one deserved by "the distraught but exciting splendor of a great failure."[14]

III *The Weakness of These Objections*

These several objections, which specify major pitfalls for a poet, are especially pertinent to a study of Crane. However, these critics apply them so flatly to his work, and they view what he was attempting so negatively that their charges need to be more carefully qualified.

Winters' accusation that Crane committed the sin of pride inherent in romanticism is unwarranted. Crane did not cherish any naïve faith in man's natural goodness and in the purity of his own instincts and emotions. A reading of Philip Horton's *Hart Crane: The Life of an American Poet*, of Crane's *Letters*, or simply of a few poems like "Recitative," "Possessions," "The Idiot," and "The Broken Tower" reveals Crane's distressed awareness of human frailty, especially his own. His record is more one of self-confessed failure than of self-righteousness and optimism. He believed in the timelessness of love, beauty, and truth and in man's hunger and capacity for them, but he was properly sceptical of the purity of his efforts to realize them.

The charge of aesthetic willfulness is more relevant and complicated. All three critics—although their terms vary—find

Crane guilty of solipsism in the creation of his poems. They contend that he placed inordinate trust in the obscure vagaries of instinct, the blind thrusts of his will, and the pressure of his sensibility. They link their criticism to his lack of any coherent system of ideas and to his willingness to violate logic.

The core of this criticism is the charge that Crane exercised no control over his work. It is that, as Blackmur wrote, he lacked any means of certifying the promptings of his Muse, any way of distinguishing between the right and wrong use of his talent. In terms of a check supplied by discursive reason or by a structure of ideas, this criticism is just. Nevertheless, it is not true that Crane had no aesthetic control at all. As we have seen, he had an internal one, one that expressed itself exclusively through his personal awareness but which he believed to be gratuitous and objective. This check was creative intuition, the ecstatic experience that initiated and controlled his artistry.

Crane's respect for his intuitive experience and his determination to express it faithfully account for his attitude toward reason. He bore no grudge against the intellect nor did he carelessly defy its laws. Actually, most of his poems have an underlying coherence, even though their imagery may at first seem totally obscure. However, there are some, like "Voyages II, III, IV," "Lachrymae Christi," "The Wine Menagerie," and "Legend" that will not yield to the analysis of discursive reason. In these he violated logic not by choice but by what he felt to be necessity. The intuitive revelation that prompted these poems was held in harmony by an organizing force distinct from logic. Crane believed that it came from a level of reality deeper than, but not in contradiction to, reason. It possessed a unity of its own—this unity was an essential feature of the experience—that he was bound to articulate despite its incompatibility with even his own ordinary standards of rationality.

Crane's attitude toward obscurity was similarly determined. He placed no intrinsic value upon it whatsoever. As he told Allen Tate, "I have always been working hard for a more perfect lucidity, and it never pleases me to be taken as wilfully obscure or esoteric."[15] His letters record his willingness to explicate his poems and his delight when readers understood them. Yet, as with his deviations from logic, there were times when he could be true to the clarity of his intuition only by being initially obscure to readers who had not experienced it. Shadows had to be admitted since they were a part of the total harmony of his creative vision. Without them the poem would have been false.

These facts about Crane's aesthetic experience and his understanding of its significance modify the general charges that have been brought against him: narcissistic willfulness, deliberate irrationality, and unnecessary obscurity. They show him to have been an artist aware of the problems involved in his work but compelled to handle them in the only way that gave meaning to his creative experience.

It is, of course, against Crane's faith in the fundamental objectivity of his creative intuition that the strictures of his critics have been aimed. In general they have agreed with Yvor Winters' elegiac conclusion: "It may seem a hard thing to say of that troubled and magnificent spirit, Hart Crane, that we shall remember him chiefly for his having shown us a new mode of damnation."[16] Winters calls this mode "romantic decadence"; what he means by it has already been summarized.

This antiromantic viewpoint is inflexibly negative. It unfairly dismisses as a delusion the belief that poetry can be based upon a nonrational intuition of objective reality. Its weakness is that it sees dangers as unavoidable and therefore cannot admit the possibility of success. The attempt to grasp reality intuitively is surely liable to the temptations that Winters and Tate mention. Self-conceit, presumption, the confusion of disorder and illumination, and the wanton indulgence of irrationality may mask themselves as creative epiphanies. However, these errors are not inevitable—as anyone who has read Crane's "Voyages" knows. These poems defy dismissal as unwitting testaments of delusion. Their unmistakable harmony and radiance can be accounted for only if they are seen as Crane saw them—as expressions of gratuitous intuition.

The animus of the antiromantic position is its anxious regard for rationality. Winters, Tate, and Blackmur fear that a poetic based upon an inspiration deeper than reason and, consequently, refusing any obligation to rational standards invites irresponsibility. They are so aware of man's liability to self-deception and disorder that they fear the worst whenever reason is not clearly served. Winters expresses this concern in the extreme demand he makes of poetry: "The poem is good insofar as it makes a defensible rational statement about a given human experience . . . and at the same time communicates the emotion which ought to be motivated by that rational understanding of the experience."[17] Blackmur, too, feels the same foreboding when, as has been seen, he points out that poetry entirely dependent upon the demon of inspiration lacks any power of self-criticism. He is afraid of exposing poetry to anarchy, and he is unwilling to encourage an effort that runs this risk.

The insistence of these critics upon rationality suggests the irony that they are not at all confident of its metaphysical status. Like the person who, because he is dubious of virtue, suspects vice everywhere, these critics show signs of a radical scepticism. They seem to regard reason not as a condition of the inner life of things but, on the contrary, as a desperate stay against fundamental disorder. Because they doubt the rationality of those human experiences that are not in conformity with the premises of discursive reason, they cannot condone a non-rational aesthetic.

Such unwillingness limits the responsiveness of these critics to poetry, and it accounts for their readiness to reject the notion of the objectivity of creative intuition because such a premise might encourage irresponsibility. They place themselves in the role of literary puritans eager to frustrate the development of any human faculty that they do not trust to be tractable. They censure Crane and "romantics" generally for relying upon creative intuition and for surrendering to its insights, even though these artists belong to a visionary tradition of poetry as old as Western culture.

IV *Maritain's Positive Viewpoint*

This visionary tradition has in recent times received its most comprehensive and sympathetic treatment in the work of the Thomist philosopher, Jacques Maritain. In *The Situation of Poetry*—a small volume of essays by him and his wife—and in his major work, *Creative Intuition in Art and Poetry* (1953), he has provided the necessary corrective to the distrustful, narrow view taken by Crane's critics. Maritain treats with the utmost respect the endeavor of modern poets to express their creative ecstasies. He understands their willingness to violate the precepts of discursive reason; he credits their claim of passing beyond subjective experience, and he accepts the presence of obscurity in their work as inevitable. Moreover, he extends this support from the standpoint of a rational philosophical system.

He accomplishes this reconciliation by asserting the "reasonableness" of the aesthetic experience despite its independence of logic. He writes:

Poetry has its source in the preconceptual life of the intellect. I use the words intellect and reason as synonymous, insofar as they designate a single power or faculty in the human soul. But I want to emphasize, from the start, that the very words reason or intellect, when they are related to that spiritual energy which is poetry, must be understood in a much deeper and larger sense than is usual. The intellect, as well as the imagination, is at the core of poetry. But reason, or the intellect, is not merely logical reason; it involves an exceedingly more profound—and more obscure—life, which is revealed to us in proportion as we endeavor to penetrate the hidden recesses of poetic activity. In other words, poetry obliges us to consider the intellect both in its secret wellsprings inside the human soul and as functioning in a nonrational (I do not say antirational) or nonlogical way.[18]

Maritain's position is defined by his analysis of the source of poetry—creative intuition. Locating it in the intelligence at a point beyond and more encompassing than the grasp of discursive reason, he is prepared to find its insights too rich to be contained by logic. Nevertheless, because it springs from "those depths of the soul where intelligence and desire, intuition and sensibility, imagination and love have their common source,"[19] he trusts in its essential harmony with reason.

He asserts that the poet's experience of this preconscious region of his being is through a creative emotion which suffuses him and bears the unique knowledge contained in art. This knowledge is "an obscure grasping of his own Self and of things."[20] It is knowledge through "connaturality"; that is, experienced knowledge. The poet has lived what he knows, and a poem is the record of his experience. Maritain carefully explains that knowledge through connaturality "is not rational knowledge, knowledge through the conceptual, logical, and discursive exercise of reason. But it is really and genuinely knowledge, though obscure and perhaps incapable of giving account of itself."[21]

Although the poet's pre- or un-conscious life is the source of creative intuition, Maritain insists that this wellspring is not to be confused with the Freudian unconscious: "the unconscious of blood and flesh, instincts, tendencies, complexes, repressed images and desires, traumatic memories."[22] The Freudian unconscious is automatic and its revelations are entirely subjective, but the unconscious that animates art is spiritual, a current of the divine soul that sustains all of creation. "These two kinds of unconscious life are in intimate connection and ceaseless communication with one another,"[23] but they must be distinguished if the mysterious penetration of the artist's subjective being by the knowledge contained in creative intuition is to be recognized.

Maritain's explanation of the source and significance of creative intuition makes the discipline of the poet and the presence of obscurity in his work more comprehensible. The artist is not a free agent. The cost of his passive reception of intuition is his unremitting effort to articulate it. His duty is to make his expression adequate to his inspiration. Until this is done, his experience is incomplete and to that extent unknown. His standard is the intuitive experience itself; the clarity of his work is determined by its congruence to this source. Since his experience comes from preconscious reaches of the soul, it is inevitable that his work will be somewhat obscure. As Raissa Maritain explains, "The sense of the unsoundable mystery of things, the revelation, the discovery of unwonted analogies, the desire to express, come what may, the ineffable, are the positive and transcendental causes of the obscurity in poetry."[24]

The Maritains' sympathetic and careful analysis of nonrational creative intuition provides a positive approach to Crane's poetry. They discuss philosophically the opportunity that he grappled with personally and poetically. Their helpfulness is that they are as aware of its temptations as are Crane's suspicious critics; yet they are persuaded of its dignity and value. In the light of their perspicacity, it is easier to do Crane justice.

CHAPTER 7

Evaluation

HAVING DISCUSSED Crane's view of poetry, his principal themes, his three major poems, and the most influential critics of his work, there remains the question of the value of his poetry. Why is this poet important? What are the dimensions of his achievement?

Crane's poetry is important for several reasons. First, he possessed an extraordinary gift for metaphor. As stated earlier, the remembrance of single phrases or lines is the most widespread general response to Crane's work. His poems, of course, present a harmony embracing more than single images, but their greatest intensity—their brilliance—is located in particular phrases. His distinguishing trait is the pitch of eloquence that he often achieves several times in a single poem through the startling aptness of his imagery.

Poem after poem offers gems of metaphor: the Brooklyn Bridge as "unfractioned idiom," the mythic Indian dancer "thewed of the levin, thunder-shod and lean," the "empty trapeze" of the burlesque dancer's flesh, "the bright logic" of poetry, the "smoked forking spires" of the city, the "unmangled target smile" of Christ. Each reader may make his own catalogue; all would document the power of an astonishing lyric imagination.

His work is significant, too, because of its irresistibly moving theme: man's quest for enduring love and absolute beauty. He expresses moods varying from exultant trust that the fulfillment of his quest is imminent to a downcast premonition of continued failure, but his desire never deviates from the true north of his idealism. This preoccupation gives a dignity and a universality to his poetry. The urgency of his yearning bestirs even readers who have convinced themselves of the futility of his desire or who have long since ceased to feel it. He awakens profound longings that men respect themselves more for having once again experienced.

Another appealing feature of Crane's poetry is its passionate involvement with life. It bespeaks his total commitment—body and soul—to human experience. He wanted love and beauty; no renunciation or sublimation was ever possible. In striving for the satisfaction of his personal hungers, he activated destructive forces that ultimately overwhelmed him, but his desire was positive and life-loving. Even when imbued with grief and failure, his longing for the attainment of full human stature is more inspiring than the expression of a life made comfortable by evasion or by lack of appetite.

These traits comprise Crane's poetic strength; they are best exemplified by his short lyrics of intimate self-revelation, like "Lachrymae Christi," "Possessions," and "Voyages." His work is less impressive when he attempts to bring society within his range. His indictment of the vulgarity of modern times is overdrawn. His acquaintance with society seems too narrow for the intensity of his criticism. Moreover, the presence of vulgarity must be assumed in all times; the test of idealism is whether or not it can flourish in spite of this handicap. Similarly, his exploration of America's past in search of encouragement for his idealism is lyrically moving but historically unconvincing. His knowledge of the past seems spotty; his judgments, self-willed.

Ironically, Crane's exhortations to hopefulness are not persuasive. Their shrillness betrays a lack of confidence. Either the evidence he offers is too weak for the pressure he puts upon it or a passage of yea-saying is followed by a more powerful passage which is frankly melancholy. Yet his poetry arouses hopefulness, not by virtue of his advocacy but because, despite all setbacks, he never loses hope himself. Crane's ability to sustain his dream in the teeth of defeat and to give eloquent expression to both his humiliation and his revival of confidence is the height of his achievement. By imaginative intensity and perfect candor, he made his unremitting quest for absolute beauty and love an exciting literary adventure.

Notes and References

Chapter One

1. Hart Crane, *The Letters of Hart Crane: 1916-1932*, ed. Brom Weber (New York, 1952), p. 8.
2. Philip Horton, *Hart Crane: The Life of an American Poet* (New York, 1937), p. 80.
3. Crane, *Letters*, pp. 108-9.
4. Horton, p. 286.
5. Crane, *Letters*, pp. 170-71.
6. Crane, *Letters*, p. 3.
7. Crane, *Letters*, p. 118.
8. Crane, *Letters*, p. 137.
9. Crane, *Letters*, p. 189.
10. "Ion," *The Works of Plato*, trans. B. Jowett (New York, n.d.), pp. 286-87.
11. Arthur Rimbaud, *Oeuvres Complètes* (Paris, 1954), p. 268.
12. Jacques Maritain, *Creative Intuition in Art and Poetry* (New York, 1953), p. 115.
13. Maritain, *Creative Intuition*, p. 119.
14. Crane, *Letters*, p. 237.
15. Crane, *Letters*, p. 90.
16. Crane, *Letters*, p. 128.
17. Malcolm Cowley, *Exile's Return: A Literary Odyssey of the 1920's* (New York, 1951), pp. 229-30.
18. Hart Crane, "General Aims and Theories," included in Horton, pp. 323-28.
19. Horton, p. 327.
20. *Ibid.*
21. Crane, *Letters*, p. 176.
22. I. A. Richards, *Science and Poetry* (New York, 1926), p. 74.
23. Ezra Pound, *Literary Essays of Ezra Pound*, ed. and intro. T. S. Eliot (Norfolk, Conn., 1954), p. xiii.
24. Pound, p. 23.
25. Pound, p. 58.
26. Pound, p. 19.
27. Ezra Pound, *The Letters of Ezra Pound, 1907-1941*, ed. D. D. Paige (New York, 1950), p. 215.
28. Pound, *Literary Essays*, p. 49.

29. Pound, *Literary Essays*, p. 54.

30. Jacques Maritain and Raissa Maritain, *The Situation of Poetry*, trans. Marshall Suther (New York, 1955), p. 42.

31. Crane, *Letters*, p. 28.

32. Crane, *Letters*, p. 71.

33. Crane, *Letters*, p. 44.

34. Crane, *Letters*, p. 90.

35. *White Buildings: Poems by Hart Crane*, foreword Allen Tate, (New York, 1926). For critical estimates of *White Buildings*, see Allen Tate, "Foreword to *White Buildings*"; also, reviews by Waldo Frank, *The New Republic*, XLIX (March 16, 1927), 116-17; Yvor Winters, *Poetry*, XXX (April, 1927), 47-51; Mark Van Doren, *The Nation*, CXXIV (February 2, 1927), 120. Tate's and Winters' commendatory remarks are especially interesting in the light of their later misgivings about *The Bridge* and Crane's work generally. Their objections are discussed at length in Chapter VI.

36. Waldo Frank, "Editor's Note," *The Collected Poems of Hart Crane* (New York, 1933), p. v. It has even been claimed by Brom Weber that what Waldo Frank assumed to be manuscript copies of these poems were actually imperfect transcriptions made by Samuel Loveman, a friend of Crane's. See Brom Weber, "Correspondence," *Poetry*, XCII (August, 1958), 332-35.

Chapter Two

1. Crane, *Letters*, p. 148.

2. Crane, *Letters*, p. 89.

3. Crane, *Letters*, p. 117.

4. Horton, p. 173.

5. For an excellent study of "Lachrymae Christi," essentially in harmony with the one presented here, see Martin Staples Shockley, "Hart Crane's 'Lachrymae Christi,' " *University of Kansas City Review*, XVI (Autumn, 1949), 31-36.

6. Crane submitted "At Melville's Tomb" to *Poetry*, and Harriet Monroe, the editor, questioned the coherence of some of his images. Crane replied by explaining his belief in a "logic of metaphor." His statement is reprinted as an appendix in Horton's *Hart Crane*, pp. 329-34, and the entire correspondence is reprinted in Brom Weber, *Hart Crane* (New York, 1948), pp. 416-22. This exchange of views is also discussed in Brooks and Warren, *Understanding Poetry* (New York, 1938), pp. 477-82.

7. Crane, *Letters*, p. 176.

8. For an interesting comparison of Keats's "Ode to a Nightingale" and Crane's "The Wine Menagerie," see Frajam Taylor, "Keats and Crane: an Airy Citadel," *Accent*, VIII (Autumn, 1947), 34-40.

9. For a splendid presentation of "The Broken Tower," see Marius Bewley, "Hart Crane's Last Poem," *Accent*, XIX (Spring, 1959), 75-85. Bewley identifies the "she" of the seventh stanza as a humble, passive part of the poet's personality rather than as a woman.

10. Crane, *Letters*, p. 396.

11. Horton, p. 294.

Chapter Three

1. Crane, *Letters*, p. 128.

2. Horton, p. 139.

3. Crane, *Letters*, pp. 128-29.

4. Crane, *Letters*, p. 89.

5. *Ibid.*

6. Van Wyck Brooks, *Three Essays on America* (New York, 1934), p. 22.

7. Brooks, p. 184.

8. *Ibid.*

9. Randolph Bourne, *The History of a Literary Radical and Other Papers*, intro. Van Wyck Brooks (New York, 1956), p. 3.

10. Waldo Frank, *Our America* (New York, 1919), p. 229.

11. Sherwood Anderson, *Letters of Sherwood Anderson*, ed. Howard Mumford Jones in association with Walter B. Rideout (Boston, 1953), p. 52.

12. Frank, p. 9.

13. Frank, p. 10.

14. Lewis Mumford, *The Golden Day: A Study in American Literature and Culture* (New York, n.d.), p. 166.

15. Crane, *Letters*, p. 117.

16. Crane, *Letters*, pp. 114-15.

17. Crane, *Letters*, p. 89.

18. For a different explication of this section, see Brom Weber, *Hart Crane* (New York, 1948), pp. 175-87. Weber indentifies the poet in Part II with Paris of Troy rather than with Faustus.

19. Crane, *Letters*, p. 89.

20. Crane, *Letters*, p. 121.

21. Crane, *Letters*, p. 115.

22. Crane, *Letters*, p. 118.

23. Crane, *Letters*, p. 129.

Chapter Four

1. Crane, *Letters*, p. 118.

2. Crane, *Letters*, p. 124.

3. Crane, *Letters*, p. 235.

4. Henry W. Wells, *The American Way of Poetry* (New York, 1943), p. 204.

5. Tate's principal discussion of *The Bridge* appears in his essay "Hart Crane,'" most readily available in the paperbound collection of his essays, *The Man of Letters in the Modern World* (New York, 1959). Winters' earliest reaction was "The Progress of Hart Crane," *Poetry*, XXXVI (June, 1930), 153-65. He discusses Crane most fully in his *In Defense of Reason* (Denver, 1947). The opinions of these two critics about Crane's poetry are discussed at length in Chapter VI.

Several other critics suggest why Crane fell short of his goal of writing an optimistic poem about contemporary America. See Howard Blake, "Thoughts on Modern Poetry," *The Sewanee Review*, XLIII (April-June, 1935), 187-96; F. Cudworth Flint, "Metaphor in Contemporary Poetry," *The Symposium*, I (July, 1930), 310-35; Paul Friedman, *"The Bridge:* A Study in Symbolism," *The Psychoanalytic Quarterly*, XXI (1952), 49-80; Brewster Ghiselin, "Bridge into the Sea,'" *Partisan Review*, XVI (July, 1949), 679-86; Barbara Herman, "The Language of Hart Crane," *The Sewanee Review*, LVIII (Winter, 1950), 52-67; Howard Moss, "Disorder as Myth: Hart Crane's *The Bridge*," *Poetry*, LXII (April, 1943), 32-45.

The Bridge is credited with possessing a unity of imagery and structure in Stanley K. Coffman, Jr., "Symbolism in *The Bridge*," *PMLA*, LXVI (March, 1951), 65-77, and Bernice Slote, "The Structure of Hart Crane's *The Bridge*," *University of Kansas City Review*, XXIV (March, 1958), 225-38.

The only book-length study of *The Bridge* is L. S. Dembo, *Hart Crane's "Sanskrit Charge"* (Ithaca, N.Y., 1960). Dembo considers the poem "a romantic lyric given epic implications" in which Crane tries to use the circumstances of contemporary America as a way to the Absolute.

6. Tate, *Man of Letters*, p. 290.

7. For a discussion of how some critics have held *The Bridge* to an inappropriate standard, see Oscar Cargill, "Hart Crane and His Friends," *The Nation*, CLXXXVI (February 15, 1958), 142-43.

8. Crane, *Letters*, p. 125.

9. Crane, *Letters*, *p.* 223.

10. Crane, *Letters*, p. 274.

11. Crane, *Letters,* p. 305.
12. Crane, *Letters,* p. 309.
13. Crane, *Letters,* p. 353.
14. Winters, *In Defense of Reason,* p. 591.
15. Crane, *Letters,* p. 236.
16. Crane, *Letters,* p. 351.
17. Crane, *Letters,* p. 305.
18. Charles Feidelson, Jr., *Symbolism and American Literature* (Chicago, 1953).
19. Edgar Allan Poe, *Selected Writings of Edgar Allan Poe,* ed. Edward H. Davidson (Boston, 1956), pp. 469-70.
20. Emily Dickinson, *Poems by Emily Dickinson,* eds. Martha Dickinson Bianchi and Alfred Leete Hampson (Boston, 1937), pp. 195-96.
21. Herman Melville, *Pierre or, the Ambiguities* (New York, n.d.), p. 296.
22. Crane, *Letters,* p. 305.
23. Crane, *Letters,* p. 270.

Chapter Five

1. Crane, *Letters,* p. 125.
2. Crane, *Letters,* p. 148.
3. Crane, *Letters,* pp. 181-82.
4. Crane, *Letters,* p. 192.
5. For a discussion of Crane's echoes of Melville in these lines and of his relationship to Melville generally, see Joseph Warren Beach, "Hart Crane and *Moby Dick,*" *The Western Review,* XX (Spring, 1956), 183-96.
6. Crane, *Letters,* p. 317.

Chapter Six

1. Winters, p. 8.
2. Winters, p. 53.
3. R. P. Blackmur, *Form and Value in Modern Poetry* (Garden City, 1957), p. 269.
4. Ralph Waldo Emerson, "The Poet," *Selections from Ralph Waldo Emerson,* ed. Stephen E. Whicher (Boston, 1957), p. 235.
5. Winters, p. 55.
6. Winters, pp. 248-49.
7. Winters, p. 598.

8. Winters, p. 246.
9. Tate, p. 283.
10. Tate, p. 293.
11. *Ibid.*
12. Blackmur, p. 273.
13. *Ibid.*
14. *Ibid.,* p. 285.
15. Crane, *Letters,* p. 176.
16. Winters, p. 101.
17. Winters, p. 11.
18. Maritain, *Creative Intuition,* p. 4.
19. Maritain, *The Situation of Poetry,* p. 14.
20. Maritain, *Creative Intuition,* p. 115.
21. Maritain, *Creative Intuition,* p. 117.
22. Maritain, *Creative Intuition,* p. 91.
23. Maritain, *Creative Intuition,* p. 92.
24. Maritain, *The Situation of Poetry,* p. 11.

Selected Bibliography

PRIMARY SOURCES

White Buildings: Poems by Hart Crane. Foreword by Allen Tate. New York: Boni and Liveright, 1926.

The Bridge. Paris: The Black Sun Press, 1930.

The Bridge. New York: Horace Liveright, 1930.

The Collected Poems of Hart Crane. Edited with an Introduction by Waldo Frank. New York: Liveright Publishing Corp., 1933.

The Complete Poems of Hart Crane. Edited with a Foreword by Waldo Frank. Garden City, N.Y.: Doubleday Anchor Books, 1958.

The Letters of Hart Crane: 1916-1932. Edited by Brom Weber. New York: Hermitage House Inc., 1952.

Rowe, H. D. *Hart Crane: A Bibliography.* Denver: Alan Swallow, 1955. Publication data about Crane's work and a listing of critical studies.

"Special Manuscript Collection." Special Collections Library, Columbia University. Letters to and from Crane, early manuscript versions of some poems, and miscellaneous personal effects.

Weber, Brom. *Hart Crane: A Biographical and Critical Study.* New York: The Bodley Press, 1948. Appendices contain thirteen published poems not included in *The Collected Poems,* fifteen poems found among Crane's manuscripts that are not in *The Collected Poems,* seven prose reviews by Crane, and several early worksheet versions of the "Atlantis" section of *The Bridge.*

SECONDARY SOURCES

Works about Crane:

Blackmur, R. P. *Form and Value in Modern Poetry.* Garden City, N.Y.: Doubleday Anchor Books, 1957. In "New Thresholds, New Anatomies," Crane's power of revitalizing words through metaphor is praised, but misgivings are expressed about his nonrational poetic.

Dembo, L. S. *Hart Crane's "Sanskrit Charge": A Study of The Bridge.* Ithaca, N.Y.: Cornell University Press, 1960. An analysis of *The Bridge* emphasizing Crane's effort to use the circumstances of modern America as a way to the Absolute.

FOWLIE, WALLACE. *The Clown's Grail: A Study of Love in Its Literary Expression.* London: Dennis Dobson, 1947. Crane is associated with Rimbaud as a type of the alienated modern artist who employs his unrequited search for harmony and love as his principal subject.

HOFFMAN, FREDERICK J. *The Twenties: American Writing in the Postwar Decade.* New York: The Viking Press, 1955. *The Bridge* is discussed as one of the most powerful expressions of the cultural conflicts arising out of World War I.

HORTON, PHILIP. *Hart Crane: The Life of an American Poet.* New York: W. W. Norton & Co., 1937. Available now in a Compass Books paperbound edition. The most thorough presentation of Crane's life.

QUINN, SISTER M. BERNETTA. *The Metamorphic Tradition in Modern Poetry.* New Brunswick: Rutgers University Press, 1955. Crane is associated with the tendency among modern poets to overcome the oppressiveness of materialism by giving the freest rein to the intuitions of metaphor.

TATE, ALLEN. *The Man of Letters in the Modern World: Selected Essays, 1928-1955.* New York: Meridian Books, 1955. In "Hart Crane" and "Crane: The Poet as Hero," Crane's lyric power, artistic integrity, and intellectual and moral disorder are emphasized.

WAGGONER, HYATT HOWE. *The Heel of Elohim: Science and Values in Modern American Poetry.* Norman: University of Oklahoma Press, 1950. A sympathetic presentation of Crane's efforts to demonstrate the importance of poetic intuitions in a technological society.

WEBER, BROM. *Hart Crane: A Biographical and Critical Study.* New York: The Bodley Press, 1948. Supplement to Horton's biography and a pioneering critical study.

WINTERS, YVOR. *In Defense of Reason.* Denver: University of Denver Press, 1947. Crane is presented as a splendid lyricist who suffered the worst consequences of the romantic traits of irrationality and self-will.

General Works:

ANDERSON, SHERWOOD. *Letters of Sherwood Anderson.* Edited by Howard Mumford Jones in association with Walter B. Rideout. Boston: Little, Brown & Co., 1953. Testimony to the ardor in the 1920's for literary artistry and cultural reform.

BOURNE, RANDOLPH. *The History of a Literary Radical and Other Papers.* Introduction by Van Wyck Brooks. New York: S. A.

Russell, 1956. Campaign literature for the formation of a youth movement to promote a more humanistic national culture.

BROOKS, VAN WYCK. *Three Essays on America.* New York: E. P. Dutton & Co., 1934. An extremely influential indictment of materialism in America and a plea for a regeneration of a mature idealistic spirit.

COLERIDGE, SAMUEL TAYLOR. *Biographia Literaria.* Edited with an Introduction by George Watson. New York: E. P. Dutton & Co., 1956. The classic statement for modern times of the dignity and importance of the creative imagination.

COWLEY, MALCOLM. *Exile's Return: A Literary Odyssey of the 1920's.* New York: The Viking Press, 1951. An account of creative artists in the 1920's, particularly the American expatriates and their European comrades.

ELIOT, T. S. *Selected Essays.* New York: Harcourt, Brace & Co., 1950. The most important discussions in our time of poetry and literary values.

EMERSON, RALPH WALDO. *Selections from Ralph Waldo Emerson.* Edited by Stephen E. Whicher. Boston: Houghton, Mifflin Co., 1957. The pioneering American formulation of the transcendental outlook held by Crane.

FEIDELSON, JR., CHARLES. *Symbolism and American Literature.* Chicago: University of Chicago Press, 1953. A demonstration that the unifying element among the major American writers of the nineteenth century is a symbolistic attitude toward life and language.

FRANK, WALDO. *Our America.* New York: Boni & Liveright, 1919. A presentation of the potentiality in American life for the growth of idealism.

KRUTCH, JOSEPH WOOD. *The Modern Temper.* New York: Harcourt, Brace & Co., 1929. A presentation of the sceptical and materialistic viewpoint prevalent in our time.

LEWIS, R. W. B. *The American Adam: Innocence, Tragedy, and Tradition in the Nineteenth Century.* Chicago: University of Chicago Press, 1955. A presentation of the conflict in America during the nineteenth century between faith in the natural innocence and perfectibility of man and the consciousness of man's fallen nature.

MARITAIN, JACQUES. *Creative Intuition in Art and Poetry.* New York: Pantheon Books, 1953. A detailed philosophical defense of the validity of artistic intuition as objective knowledge.

MARITAIN, JACQUES AND RAISSA. *The Situation of Poetry.* Translated by Marshall Suther. New York: Philosophical Library, 1955. A brief presentation of the major judgments of *Creative Intuition in Art and Poetry.*

MUMFORD, LEWIS. *The Golden Day: A Study in American Literature and Culture.* New York: W. W. Norton & Co., n.d. Americans are urged to align themselves with the idealistic tradition found in the major American writers of the mid-nineteenth century as a way of strengthening themselves for battle with contemporary materialism.

PLATO. *The Works of Plato.* Translated by B. Jowett. New York: The Dial Press, n.d. "Ion" and "Phaedrus" are the foundation pieces in our culture for the visionary theory of poetic composition.

POUND, EZRA. *The Letters of Ezra Pound.* Edited by D. D. Paige. New York: Harcourt, Brace & Co., 1950. An invaluable account of the literary life of the twentieth century.

————. *Literary Essays of Ezra Pound.* Edited with Introduction by T. S. Eliot. Norfolk: New Directions, 1954. Lessons in literary history intended to enrich contemporary achievement and to reaffirm the importance of art.

RICHARDS, I. A. *Science and Poetry.* New York: W. W. Norton & Co., 1926. Poetry is judged inferior to science as a vehicle of knowledge.

WHITEHEAD, ALFRED NORTH. *Science and the Modern World.* New York: Macmillan Co., 1948. An attack upon the absolutism of scientific materialism and a recommendation that life be viewed as an interrelationship between mind and matter in which aesthetic intuitions are especially significant.

WHITMAN, WALT. *The Poetry and Prose of Walt Whitman.* Edited by Louis Untermeyer. New York: Simon & Schuster, 1949. The poet most influential in forming Crane's affirmative personal and cultural outlook.

Index

DATE DUE

MAY 21 '7	MAY 15 '71		
MAY 14 '72	MAY 21 '72		
NOV 6 '72	OCT 24 '72 24 '72		
GAYLORD			PRINTED IN U.S.A.